KU-181-722

MATHEMATICAL MODEL BUILDING IN ECONOMICS AND INDUSTRY

Being the collected papers of a conference
organized by C-E-I-R Ltd and held
in London on 4th to 6th July 1967

GRIFFIN · LONDON

Copyright © 1968

CHARLES GRIFFIN & COMPANY LIMITED
42 DRURY LANE, LONDON, W.C.2

SBN: 85264 106 0

Copyright in the book as a whole is vested in
Charles Griffin & Company Ltd. Copyright in the
individual papers, with one exception, is vested
in C-E-I-R Ltd. Copyright in the paper "Models
of Fact; Examples from Marketing" is vested in
Mr A. S. C. Ehrenberg.

First published . . . 1968

HB71 C6
251770.

Set by Josée Utteridge

Printed in Great Britain by
Butler & Tanner Ltd, Frome and London

6 00 142545 5   TELEPEN

Students and External Readers	Staff & Research Students
DATE DUE FOR RETURN	**DATE OF ISSUE**
	23 1277

MODEL BUILDING
IN ECONOMICS
AND INDUSTRY

OTHER BOOKS ON STATISTICS AND MATHEMATICS

PREFACE

As operations in business, industry and government become increasingly complex, so too do the mechanisms needed to control them. 'Experience' or 'intuition', though important, cannot be relied upon to provide the sole basis on which this control can sensibly be exercised. There must be some more fundamental and objective means of getting to grips with the underlying principles of the operations involved.

The building of mathematical models is rapidly becoming one of the most important methods of studying the behaviour of complicated systems and forecasting their future. The creation of such models is giving valuable insight into many complex areas of economics and industry. Problems currently being tackled range from macro-economic models of complete national economies to relatively small models of specific industrial processes.

Model building is not a precisely defined subject. It is more a method of approach to practical problems. There are a number of mathematical and computational techniques which are particularly relevant to model building, but these are the tools of the subject, and not the subject itself.

In order to draw together some of the experience gained in the field of model building, C-E-I-R Limited invited a number of leading world experts in the field to present papers at a conference entitled 'Model Building in Economics and Industry', held in London in July 1967. The object of this conference was to hear accounts from these experts of their experience in the development of models in their own area, and of their plans for the future of these models. The emphasis was on practicality.

The papers given covered a wide area of applications and dealt with many of the problems which had to be faced. It is the full text of these papers that is contained in this book. No attempt has been made to summarize them or to edit them. They were prepared independently, and some differences of opinion among authors might have been expected. It is, however, noticeable, and heartening, that there is on the whole agreement on most of the major issues, the problems encountered, and the methods of overcoming them.

We believe that this collection will be of general interest to workers,

PREFACE

not only in industry and commerce, but in much wider fields in which model building is becoming an important subject for study. It is our intention to hold further conferences of a similar kind from time to time.

London, 1968   A.M.W.

CONTENTS

MODEL BUILDING AND ITS PROBLEMS

M. G. KENDALL

The definition of model

1   In recent years the word 'model' has been used, or mis-used, to describe almost any attempt at specifying a system under study. There will be differences of opinion about what kinds of specification we permit to constitute a model in the scientific sense. I do not wish to enter into much discussion about matters of definition — it is usually a sign of insecurity to argue overmuch about fundamentals — but we should, perhaps, begin this conference with some account of the nature of the subject.

2   A 'model' does not necessarily, or even usually, mean some physical replica of the system, in the sense that an aircraft designer constructs a model so as to study its behaviour in a wind-tunnel or an astronomer builds an orrery. Sometimes our models are indeed physical machines, and there are even cases (such as Professor Phillips' early hydrodynamic model of an economic system) in which a set of non-physical relationships are imitated by a physical system. But for the most part we mean by 'model' a specification of the inter-relationships of the parts of a system, in verbal or mathematical terms, sufficiently explicit to enable us to study its behaviour under a variety of circumstances and, in particular, to control it and to predict its future.

3   A glance at the current journals will indicate the wide range of subjects now relying on model building and analysis. I take the following examples more or less at random from the published literature of the last few years :

(a) Parks' (1964) study of the generation and control of forest fires in California.

(b) A study by Kilbridge and Webster (1966) on the optimum division of labour along a continuous assembly line in a factory.

(c) A study by Dill, Gaver, and Weber (1965) on the progression of employees through various grades of promotion in a hierarchy.

(d) A group of studies (Cootner, ed. 1964) on the behaviour of the stock market; and some related studies by Markovitz (1959) and Fama (1965) on portfolio analysis.

1

(e) Fox's study (1965) of cloud formation.

(f) Sundry articles such as that by Gani and Yeo (1965) on phaze reproduction.

(g) Horvath's (1966) study of the formation of social groups.

(h) Studies by Charnes and others (1965) and by Keller (1965) on the marketing of new products.

One could extend this list almost indefinitely. There is hardly any branch of science or of industry which is not coming under the model-builder's eye.

4   Now it is not obvious that all these different applications rest on a common body of theory or a common collection of skills. We do not yet know whether it is possible to write a book on 'The Theory of Model Building'. On the face of it, however, there does exist a set of basic problems, and the necessity for a basic expertise, which are shared by all model-building exercises. For this conference we need not, and indeed could not, survey the whole field. Our interest is being limited to models in a broad economic sense, in industry, commerce, and economic systems, and I think we shall find that, regardless of country, regardless of the scope of the model, the problems and the expertise required to resolve them do constitute a unified subject. At any rate, that is one of the things we hope to find out.

Models and decisions

5   There is one important preliminary point for clarification. The word 'model' may suggest that we are attempting to construct a microcosm of the system in the sense that the model will mimic the behaviour of its macro-counterpart in all respects. This is not so. The systems we have to study are far too complicated to permit of anything of the kind and we shall find, I think, that we are continually having to curb an ambition which tempts us to build models of too great a generality. Or, to put it another way, we build models for specific purposes, not for all possible purposes. The first question to ask when we embark on the construction of a model is : what am I going to do with it when I have it ? Or, to put it in still another way, the manner in which we construct a model depends on the decisions which it is ultimately going to help us to make. One consequence of this is that we may have quite different models of the same system for different purposes. A model of a company for the purpose of planning capital investment may be very different from a model of the same company for planning its system of information flow, and both would differ from a model of manpower requirements.

6   I myself I am inclined to go further — I throw this out for general consideration — and to suggest that model building should start with

simple and modest models, and work towards the more complicated systems by integration, rather than start with attempts at comprehensive models. There are dangers here — there are dangers everywhere in this subject. An over-simplification may fail to mimic the system adequately enough. And the layman is fully entitled to distrust a crude model which leaves out of account features of the system which he knows to exist and believes to be important. But I think the resolution of this particular difficulty lies very largely with a full realisation of the point I have just made — the object of the model is not to imitate for the sake of imitation, but to enable certain decisions to be taken; and the question is whether what we omit in a simplified model is relevant to the decision, not to the accuracy of the representation.

7   There are, of course, models which are nothing more than explanatory of the anatomy of a system. In this sense a map is a model of the area to which it relates, a flow diagram is a model of a systematic logical procedure; and the organisation chart of a company, notwithstanding that it is always out of date and is often honoured more in the breach than the observance, is, in this limited sense, a model of the company. I suggest that we admit these static structural pictures of the situation as models in our sense — the name 'iconic' has been proposed for them. Very often they are an essential preliminary to the construction of a working model. But for purposes of control and prediction we are concerned with much more than a static representation, however useful that may be. We have to consider, in some sense or other, the movement of the system and thus our models are almost always dynamic.

Classification of models

8   It would be useful if we could have some system of classification of the various types of model we have to consider. Perhaps it is premature to attempt such a system at the present stage of development but it will clarify ideas if I mention some possible dichotomies, even if they involve cross-classification:

(a) *Deterministic versus stochastic models*

In some cases we write down equations expressing the behaviour of the system in purely deterministic terms. This is common in physics but not so common in the social sciences. For example, Parks' model of forest fires is purely deterministic. So is that of Kilbridge and Webster on the progressive assembly line. More usually, especially in economics, we have to admit a stochastic element, that is to say, some of our variables are random in the sense that the actual values emerge from the chaos of predestination like the falls of dice or the spins of a roulette wheel. Extreme cases of purely stochastic models are rare — the model of stock market movements as a random walk is a case in point — and nearly all the models we shall be concerned with are mixed determino-stochastic models. Sometimes we have stochastic behaviour on a deterministic system, like the random patterns of traffic on a fixed network; sometimes our system itself is partly stochastic.

(b) *Solvability versus simulation*

For systems of a fairly simple kind (and sometimes with sufficient mathematical skill, for more complicated systems) it is possible to solve the equations of motion explicitly and to exhibit the behaviour in the shape of general formulae. This, of course, is the mathematician's ideal. More often it happens that we can write down the equations but cannot solve them; or that there are too many unknowns; or that the system is so complex than an attempt to write it down in detail would frustrate the whole inquiry. In such circumstances we can very often simulate the behaviour of the system under a set of different assumptions and, as it were, form a picture of its behaviour by sampling from all the ways it might behave. If solvability is wanting, simulation provides the second line of attack.

(c) *Descriptive versus analytic models*

Some models attempt only to set up stimulus-response relationships for the system without probing into the reasons for their existence. To test a car driver's reactions we need only apply a set of stimuli and observe the delay in response without stopping to enquire into the neural mechanism which connects the two. This may not tell us much about human physiology, or how to improve his skill, but it may be enough to tell us whether he should be allowed to drive. In current jargon the system is a 'black box' and we are content to study the input-output relations without taking the lid off the box and trying to find out how it works. A great deal of short-term prediction is of this character.

Sooner or later, however, we want to look inside the box, not merely out of curiosity, but because we want to know how the system would behave if some of its determinant relations were changed. A model which attempts to describe the behaviour inside the box may be called 'analytic'. All econometric models are analytic to some extent.

The distinction between descriptive and analytic models however, is one of degree rather than of kind. For example, if we are constructing a model of a heat engine, it may be sufficiently analytic to regard the pressure-volume-temperature relations of a gas as represented by Boyle's law, Charles' law, or various physical modifications of them. For the molecular physicist, however, these relations may be of the black-box type expressing the statistical properties of molecular motions and collisions in which he is interested. The point becomes of particular importance in macro-economic models, in which we are often compelled by paucity of data or sheer complexity or even sheerer ignorance to substitute aggregative relations for collections of individual relations. The best way of looking at the matter, I think, is to regard the model-building process as a continuing attempt to become more and more analytic, starting with a simple model which may be only descriptive and penetrating more and more into the causal relationships as knowledge and experience accrue. This, after all, is the traditional approach of the scientist.

9 There are other distinctions which can be drawn between different classes of model, e.g. short-term and long-term models, according to the period of prediction for which they are to be used; computable or noncomputable, according to whether the model is sufficiently explicit to enable an electronic computer to be programmed for numerical study of its behaviour; macro- versus micro-models, according to the breadth of the scope of the model or the degree of aggregation in the formulation of its basic relations. At the present stage of development we need not worry too much about a complete system of classification so long as we understand what these distinctions imply.

Problems of model building

10 I now proceed to describe what, in my opinion, are the main problems of model building and analysis. For the most part what is said below applies to all kinds of models, but the construction of economic and social models has some special problems of its own to which I shall call particular attention. Two preliminary comments:

(a) The model is only as good as the raw material to which it is applied. We all know the extreme difficulties of getting good data in economics: the large amount of error in some of the estimates; delays in the production of some of the figures; changes in the basis of periodic figures such as index numbers; the relatively short time periods for which comparable information is available. I do not minimize the problems of data collection, but they are not my direct concern in this introductory paper.

(b) If one makes a list of all the difficulties which face the economic model builder, it becomes so frighteningly long as to scare many people off the subject. This is the very reverse of my intention. I should, therefore, like the remaining part of this paper to be regarded as the specification of a programme of research rather than a plaintive exposition of how difficult it all is. We obviously have a long way to go before we solve our problems, and perhaps some rather traumatic experiences in reshaping our fundamental thinking about them. But we cannot afford to throw in our hands.

Variables

11 The first problem concerns the nature of the variables with which we are to deal. In the physical sciences this is not usually serious. Everything is expressible in terms of units of length, time, mass and electric charge with, perhaps, a few ad hoc concepts such as electronic spin. Moreover, these units are well defined, do not vary over time, and can be measured with exquisite precision. Sometimes we introduce concepts like force which are not directly observable, but always in such a way that the model can be verified by readings in terms of the fundamental units.

In economics, sociology and psychology we are not in such a fortunate position. We are forced to think in terms of value, or utility, or demand, for example, and have to recognize that even if these concepts are quantifiable, there is something essentially subjective about them. The only common units are weight, which is in any case inapplicable to services, or money, which fluctuates in value. Our yardsticks of measurement are therefore elastic. We can and do attempt to bring our time-series to comparability by correcting for changes in the value of money ; but the value of money is itself a rather sophisticated concept. Even with models of manpower, where our primary units are countable human beings, we have to have some regard to quality if we are to be at all realistic.

12 The question then arises whether we should admit into our models quantities which are essentially non-observable. I myself see no reason why we should not, just as we admit non-observables into the equations of physics, but I do think that we should be careful not to reify concepts which may have no validity. For example, in setting up a model of demand, should I admit a variable 'propensity to consume' if I can think of no way of measuring it ? We hear a great deal about 'productive capacity' nowadays; but is the expression clear enough for us to allow it to define a basic variable ?

Relations among variables

13 Early attempts to formalize economic relations in mathematical terms were nearly all expressed in terms of functional relationships. Moreover, they were of a static kind, in the sense that, for example, we would write demand d in terms of price p as

$$d = f(p)$$

without reference to time-lags or the transient phase required for a change in price to exert its full effect on demand. As systems became more complicated, and more variables were brought into equations, the relationships were usually simplified into linear expressions. It was fully appreciated that linearity was approximative, but the belief was that, in the range likely to be encountered in practice, the approximation would be reasonably close to observed behaviour.

14 We still, for the most part, deal with linear equations, partly, it must be admitted, because linear mathematics are the only easy mathematics and partly because we can always argue that any curve is nearly linear in a small enough range. But we have moved from the purely deterministic model to a stochastic model by admitting random variables into the equations. This raises problems of identifiability in that we may write down a model in which certain constants cannot be estimated, however many observations we have, unless we introduce extraneous information. It also raises some severe problems of statistical estimation (an account of different methods of handling sets of stimultaneous linear stochastic equations is given by Fisk (1967)).

15 However, before we come to the problem of solving our system, there are two further points to be noticed.

First, some of our relations governing the system may be inequalities rather than equalities. In fact, some models of an industrial plant, such as an oil refinery, may consist almost entirely of constraints expressing, for example, the maximum capacity of intake or minimum requirements in output to meet contractual obligations. The theory of mathematical programming has been constructed during the past twenty years to deal with such situations. When we have a mixed system comprising equalities of a deterministic or stochastic kind together with constraints of the inequality type, the formal solution of our relations may become very complicated indeed and I would not like to say that the subject has yet been mastered. So far as I know, not very much has been done in macro-economic models to deal with the situation: for example, in some kinds of relationship (such as a linear equation of price in terms of demand) we may expect one of the coefficients to be negative if it is to make sense as an elasticity; or in some stochastic models certain of the quantities under estimate, being probabilities, must be positive.

Time-lags

16 Second, and more important still, we have now realised that the behaviour of economic systems depends critically on the time-lags between stimulus and response. Classical economics, when it got as far as expressing its relations in mathematical terms, did so in the manner of the equation in paragraph 13, as a static relation. To deduce the dynamic behaviour of a system from such equations was as impossible as to deduce the laws of planetary motion from the triangle of forces, which accounts for the fact that the mathematical formulation added little or nothing to economic theory. Nowadays it is appreciated by econometricians that time plays an essential role, especially in the feedback systems.

17   Now this raises a whole host of problems. It has now been shown (Professor Stone does it in simple terms) that the very stability of a system may depend on time-lags, which thus assume a fundamental role in the structure of the model. Again, the length of a lag, or the pattern of a transient phase from the initial application of a stimulus to its final equilibrium, are among the most difficult of economic effects to measure, and it is surprising how little we know about them even in the best documented economies. How long, for example, does an alteration in the bank rate take to exert its full effect, and how far does production lag behind unemployment, or unemployment behind production? Added to such difficulties we have the practical problems arising from the nature of economic data : if, for example, a system is so highly responsive as to react in a matter of days or weeks, a model which has to rely on monthly or quarterly data may miss some basic reactions.

18   There are ways of tackling these problems. Where the system is being observed at intervals which are too coarse to permit of a satis- factory model we may have to conduct ad hoc enquiries on a finer mesh. There are some interesting mathematical problems here, as to how fine a mesh should be, and whether it would pay to have varying intervals of observation rather than a uniform spacing. Again, with modern statistical methods developed on the computer we can make a good deal of progress in estimating the approximate length of lags between given variables. It appears also, as in some short-term forecasting models, that the results we get are relatively insensitive to assumptions made about certain parts of the system, which leads us on to a new branch of the subject, sensiti- vity analysis (or how rough and ready can I be without impairing the re- liability of my final conclusions ?).

19   In passing, let us note one point connected with the collection of primary data. With a few exceptions, models built up to the present have had to rely on statistics produced by Government Departments, or central authorities of some kind, for quite different purposes. If Government is going to become seriously interested in model building there will arise the necessity for collecting data for that purpose in itself, which may have a far-reaching effect on the nature of the State's statistical service. Even in such a construct as an input-output table, which is an instantaneous snapshot of an economy and is not complicated by time-effects (or not very much so) the amount of work which has been necessary to compile the raw data is enormous compared to the time required to apply it.

20 To revert to the question of time-lags, we may also observe that it raises a new class of problem for the statistician and even for the philosopher. The statistician, accustomed to dealing with stochastic systems, has developed some highly sophisticated methods of estimation and testing hypotheses and we still find some of the elementary texts speaking of the standard errors of a forecast, or confidence belts surrounding a prediction, as if the uncertainties surrounding model building were the same sort of uncertainties that we get when we have to draw inferences from a random sample. They are not; or rather, sampling uncertainty is only a part of the error which we may incur. There is the error of choosing the wrong model; the error of approximating by omitting relations, by aggregating or by replacing an unknown relationship by a random variable; the error forced on us by using one variable which we can measure in place of one which we should prefer but cannot measure. For the benefit of any statisticians here, let me add a technical point: it sometimes happens in more complicated cases that the likelihood surface has several modes, and I would not exclude the possibility that it may have ridges or craters, which implies that we may have some thinking to do about the accepted principles of inference.

21 I referred a few moments ago to the fact that we may have problems even for the philosopher. They arise from the nature of causality. Most of the relations detected by the statistician *by purely statistical analysis* are devoid of causational content. The standard theory of regression and correlation, for example, purports to find and to display patterns of relationships which appear quite stable and can be used for prediction but which, on the face of it, are nonsense. They are simple black box situations although in practice, of course, we can often supply a causal nexus from extraneous knowledge.

22 In feedback systems it is sometimes hard to say what is cause and what is effect, and indeed there may be relationships in which each of a pair of variables causes the other. An increase in wages, for example, may result in a call for increased production; and an increase in production may result in an increase in that part of factor remuneration which gives rise to higher wages. There is no mathematical reason why we should not write down two relationships provided there are suitable lags inserted to make sure that they are consistent. Feedback systems, in their very nature, are of this kind. Professor Wold, however, has thought about the matter along different lines by limiting the relations in a model to what he calls a 'causal chain'. I will not try to anticipate what he has to say on this subject. At this stage we may merely remark that, without getting ourselves tied up in knots over the nature of causality, we do have a problem concerning the asymmetry of relationships which we are prepared to admit into a model.

B

23 Perhaps at this stage, before we alarm ourselves at the number and magnitude of some of the problems that face us, it is as well to mention a few reassuring features.

In the first place, it is not necessarily true that the behaviour of a complicated system is itself very complicated; or to put it another way, the output variables in which we are primarily interested may have quite simple and usable patterns even if the mechanism which generated them is highly complex. Statistics is full of examples of the kind. For instance, the circumstances and motivation which go to determine an individual's income are legion, and any model which tried to set out the situation in detail would soon get bogged down in sheer complexity. Nevertheless the Pareto law of income distribution is fairly closely followed in all Western societies and depends on only one parameter. Moreover, it has proved remarkably stable over decades of fundamental change in economic controls. Or again, voting is a matter of free will if anything is, and the spectrum of political opinions on different topics is very wide. Nevertheless, the laws of voting behaviour are sufficiently well understood in the U.K. to enable election results to be predicted with remarkable accuracy. Mr. Ehrenberg may have more to say on this subject. He is himself responsible for one of the most general economic patterns yet observed, the negative binomial law governing consumers' purchases. I gave a number of others examples in my paper on 'Natural Law in the Social Sciences' (1961).

24 Thus statistical aggregation effects themselves simplify the model. It is a mistake to suppose that disaggregation necessarily improves representation or that, because a system is known to consist of a lot of small components, every item must be explicitly written into the model. It seems to me that one of the duties of the econometrician ought to be to search for these patterns of behaviour. They occur in the most unexpected quarters and, quite often, are not suggested by prior logical analysis. We could regard this facet of the econometrician's work as analogous to some aspects of the biochemist's : try everything one can think of in the hope that sooner or later some useful relation will come to light, and then see how it works and why it holds.

25 A second source of encouragement is provided by the electronic computer. I need not expatiate on this topic. We are all aware that all but the very simplest models need a computer in order to study their behaviour in real time, that is to say, quickly enough to be of any use in decision taking. It would not be an over-statement to say that econometrics and model building have only become practical possibilities since the computer was developed. Early writers had many of the ideas but the practical engineering of the subject had to wait for the technological breakthrough represented by the electronic machine. I do not believe that any of the

major problems of model building will be solved quickly and elegantly; they will have to be teased out slowly by a combination of all the skills we can bring to bear on them; and the computer will be an essential engine in the process.

26 We may also derive some comfort — not very much at the precise moment, perhaps, but more as time goes on — at the reflection that we are gradually becoming free from a major difficulty facing the economist of the past — the impossibility of experimentation. We can already experiment to some extent: for example an advertising campaign can be localized in one area which can be compared with another area where the campaign is not conducted; or we could experiment with different types of education. More importantly for our present purpose is the fact that the model is itself an instrument of experimentation. As yet we do not know much about the general behaviour of models of given types, for example whether increasing complexity necessarily, or probably, entails a tendency to oscillation or conversely, where and how to insert feedback circuits to stabilize a system with a tendency to fluctuate; or whether cyclical movements of the relaxed oscillation variety can be generated in a system where the capacity (of the stock-held type) is spread throughout rather than concentrated at particular points. Altogether apart from the construction of models for decision taking, there is a wide field open for exploration as to how certain kinds of models react to stimuli.

27 I have left until last one of the most important questions we have to face: how do we test a model? How do we know whether it is a good model? I can think of no better answer to these questions than to say that the primary test is whether the model works. In practice this usually means whether it is successful in predicting and controlling. In this I suppose we are in no different position from any scientist who, having framed a hypothesis, tests it against new data and observes the extent of agreement. But the scientist usually has plenty of new data or can collect it. One of our problems is that we don't quite know what constitutes a good agreement and in many circumstances cannot wait to accumulate experience over a period of years before using the model. (We can always test it over the past, but this is not such a convincing test, especially where we have made it fit past experience.) In defence of model builders, if they need defence, one should perhaps point out this important feature of their work, that they are often denied by the pressure of events the amount of testing which goes, for example, into the design of a new aircraft or the launching of a new drug or even the marketing of a relatively new product.

The application of models

28 I have referred to the fact that a model depends for its nature on the use to which it is put, and that its success depends on whether it 'works'. There are obviously many different kinds of use and many different criteria of working; but it may help to clarify our discussions if I draw a few distinctions:

Cases occur where the mere concept of model does much to advance our thinking about a system. To illustrate the point, let me propound a question without attempting an answer. Most businesses have a chain of command expressible by the branching pedigree type of diagram already mentioned; and this diagram, so to speak, works in both directions. Instructions flow downwards, information flows upwards, decisions at defined levels are made at various points of the network. (We already know that this may give rise to difficulty as between staff and line responsibility.) Now Nature, in designing the human being, has proceeded differently and provided at least four different systems to control the human body (arterial, venous, vascular and nervous) and has linked them in a very intricate and roundabout way. In considering the social or commercial organism ought we to take a leaf out of her book? Does it follow that the executive chain should be the same as the information chain, or the decisional system the same as the executive system? I do not know the answer, and there may not be an answer. The point I wish to make is that in thinking about a situation from the model-building viewpoint we may be led to some quite fundamental queries concerning the structure of the system under study.

29 There is also a useful distinction to be drawn between forecasting as an objective in itself, and control. A model of an economy may be useful to a firm as a forecaster of the future, in the sense that the firm wants to predict the environment in which it will find itself, not directly to control it; whereas the same model might be useful to government in the actual control of the economy. In management the primary objective, I think, is control, and the time may even come when our models are themselves controls in the sense that they automatically bring into play forces to direct the system along a chosen path, like the auto-pilot of an aircraft. There is no conflict of aim in devising these cybernetic systems; but there may be a conflict among users, in the sense that industry may want to rely on forecasts from a model whereas Government may want to falsify them. It does not seem to me that control models are essentially different in nature from forecasting models, but they may differ in kind or in emphasis, and certainly in the amount of black-box type of relation which we write into them.

30 It would have been very pleasant, in this preliminary survey of model building, to be able to say something in answer to a question which is often posed to us: how does one set about building a model? This, I suppose, is one of those general questions, like how does one design a

building, or how does one cure a disease ? — it all depends on what sort of a model and what are the uses to which it is to be put. Granting that, we are still not able to anatomize the model-building process. Perhaps, when enough of us have built enough models for enough purposes and have gained enough experience of how they work, it will be possible to lay down a course of instruction for would-be model builders and even to produce textbooks on the theory of the subject. I doubt whether we can do anything of the kind at the present time. What we can do is to compare notes, read the literature (which is already fairly extensive) and hear the experts describe their experience in running models. And that is really the object of this conference.

31   Certain facts, however, seem to me to have emerged already. In limited fields, or with limited objectives, it may be possible for one gifted individual to have at his command all the skills required to construct and test a model. But the larger models are, I think, a matter for team effort, or at least for effort on the part of an individual who has access to team support. A macro-economic model, for example, requires the analytical training of the economist, the knowledge of available data of the descriptive statistician, the expertise of the theoretical statistician and perhaps of a specialized mathematician, the skill of the machine programmer and the common sense of all of them. The moral of this seems to me to be that we are in some danger of spreading our efforts too thinly on the ground. If, as I expect, there will be a growing interest in model building over the next ten or twenty years, and the effort which can be put into the subject is limited in time, money, and intellectual capacity, it would pay us as a nation (or a more extended community) to strengthen our strong points and concentrate on setting up units for study which exceed the critical mass at which useful results are produced. The primary object of this conference is to discuss what model building is and how to do it ; but perhaps we may have time to consider how, if we are agreed that it is an important subject, its development should be encouraged.

References

[1] Parks, G.M. (1964). Development and application of a model for the suppression of forest fires. *Man. Sci.*, **10**, 760.

[2] Fox, M. (1965). A simplified model for the formation, movement and dissipation of fair weather cumulus clouds. *J. App. Prob.*, **2**, 178.

[3] Dill, W.R., Gaver, D.P., and Weber, W.L. (1965). Models and Modelling for Manpower Planning. *Man. Sci.* **13**, B-142.

[4] Cootner, P.H. (ed.) (1964). *The Random Character of Stock Market Prices*. M.I.T. Press, Cambridge, Mass.

[5] Markovitz, H. (1959). *Portfolio Selection: the efficient diversification of investments.* New York, J. Wiley & Sons.

[6] Gani, J. and Yeo, G.F. (1965). Some birth-death and mutation models for phaze reproduction. *J. App. Prob.*, **2**, 150.

[7] Kilbridge, M. and Webster, L. (1966). An economic model for the division of labor. *Man. Sci.*, **12**, B-255.

[8] Fama, E.F. (1965). Portfolio Analysis in a Stable Paretian Market. *Man. Sci.*, **11**, 404.

[9] Horvath, W.J. (1966). Stochastic models of behaviour. *Man. Sci.*, **12**, B-513.

[10] Charnes, A., Cooper, W.W., DeVoe, J.K., and Learner, P.B. Demon: a management model for new products. *Carnegie Inst. Tech. Rep. 52.*

[11] Kendall, M.G. (1961). Natural Law in the Social Sciences. *J. Roy. Statist. Soc.*, **124**, 1.

[12] Fisk, P.R. (1967). *Stochastically dependent equations* Charles Griffin & Co., London.

ECONOMETRIC MODEL BUILDING

R. J. BALL

CONTENTS

1 The development of econometrics

The history of science reflects the continual process of the creation and discovery of knowledge that usually manifests itself in the emergence of new well defined areas of thought. The social sciences have grown out of backgrounds of history and law and philosophy to form fields of study in their own right. In many European universities, for example, economics is still not considered as a separate discipline but falls in the law faculty.

Within the general field of economics itself econometrics has developed as a field of study over the last thirty years. But although the journal of the Econometric Society was started as far back as 1933, it was only during the war and its aftermath that the subject began to grow rapidly, although even here, with some notable exceptions, the bulk of the growth occurred in the United States. In fact as far as the United Kingdom is concerned it is fair to say that only in the last decade has econometric analysis made a major impact in both university teaching and research and in work conducted in official government circles.

Econometrics is concerned with measurement in economics, and its slow growth in the United Kingdom may be ascribed to the lack of any really strong empirical tradition in British economic thought. As modern economic analysis emerged from the nineteenth century under the aegis of Alfred Marshall, the battle between the theoretical and historical schools of thought on the continent obscured the importance of empirical research and problem solving in testing and formulating hypotheses about the real economic world. Theory and application tended to develop in separate compartments, with unfortunate consequences for both. The theory tended to become devoid of those features that enable theory to assist in explaining and interpreting the real world of phenomena with which we are concerned, while at the other end of the scale, applied work was regarded as the rather painful acquisition of facts with usually little analytical framework in which to interpret those facts. The applied economist so called appeared to be a world apart from the economic theorist, and small wonder since the form in which the theoretician presented his hypotheses very often gave no guide as to how those hypotheses might be tested.

In some ways the development of econometrics as a separate branch of economics is unfortunate, for it implies that there is a subject for study called economics and another called econometrics. But the most desirable state of affairs is clearly one in which theory, practice, and measurement are woven together in studying the economic environment. For measurement without theory is as dangerous as theory without measurement, and to compartmentalize either to a major extent is to risk their divorce.

Economic theory is concerned with relationships between economic variables. Theory formulates, for example, hypotheses about how consumers will react to price changes, how producers will adjust to taxes and how nations will be affected by tariff changes. In all these analyses the basic variables are in principle subject to measurement, and hypotheses for the most part give predictions of what will happen to some variables at least qualitatively consequent on changes in other variables. It is a short step from here to expressing the logic of the relationships implied by the analyses in mathematical form, which has the advantage of not only making the assumptions underlying the relationships explicit, but also of facilitating the manipulations of such relationships in order to analyse their behaviour, particularly in systems. Such manipulations of economic variables present no problem as long as the economic world is confined to the two dimensional diagram of the elementary economics text, but in dealing with economic systems any state of the system can be thought of as a vector of values of many economic variables which define a point in n-dimensional space. Once this point is reached the advantages of mathematical representation of economic laws and relationships becomes obvious.

It was always said in elementary economics texts of long standing that economic laws should be regarded not as laws in the sense of those laws that operate in the physical sciences, but rather as 'tendencies'. Thus the laws of supply and demand were interpreted as indicating what would tend to happen to price in a market on which natural economic forces would operate. The starting point of modern econometric analysis however is to postulate in a rather more precise way the statistical character of economic relationships. Mathematical analysis of economic relationships is a subject of some long standing but such analysis treats the economic system as an exact set of relationships which are manipulated accordingly. For the purposes of theoretical analysis this is for the most part a significant and fruitful simplification. But once we reach the point of testing hypotheses or using them to predict something about the real world then the simplification is open to question. The point of view of the modern econometrician is that economic relationships are the sum or product of two components, a systematic component that is susceptible to measurement which is used to 'explain' the dependent factor in the analysis, and the random component or disturbance which represents the influence of a host of small and statistically independently distributed factors whose sum can be regarded as a random variable with a well defined probability distribution. It was said in Marshall's time that economics was concerned with the study of the margin. It can be said analogously that econometric analysis is concerned with the study of random disturbances. It is this characteristic of econometrics that marks it off from mathematical economics generally, and also from other forms of economic measurement. Thus input-output or inter-industry analysis as developed by Leontief in the United States, and which forms a key part of the work carried out by Richard Stone and his associates at Cambridge, is not usually included as part of conventional econometrics. The line of distinction is from several points of view not a clear one. The point to make here is simply that econometrics is the meeting point of economic and statistical theory applied to the data with which we represent the economic environment.

This assumption about the statistical nature of economic relationships implies that the random components of economic relationships are inherent parts of the structure of such relationships. From the point of view of force casting and control of the environment it is of course highly desirable that the systematic components of relationships are large in relation to the random or stochastic components but in particular cases this is not necessarily so. This is simply an occupational hazard for the worker in this field.

2 The model-building process

For present purposes a model may be defined as a set of relationships used to represent a physical or economic process which can usually be represented in mathematical form. There seems to be no essential difference in logic between a model that is used to predict changes in the weather and an economic model that is used to predict changes in the economic climate. It is not an accident that meteorological terminology is often apparently used to describe the economic scene. There may be other reasons why one wishes to discriminate clearly between weather models and economic models, but in terms of logical structure the similarities appear more significant than the differences. In both cases the use of the word 'represent' as in the first sentence of this section must be interpreted carefully. The purpose of building a model is not to *describe* the process that is going on. Economic models as defined are often criticised as being unrealistic, partly because of a belief (or perhaps a wish) that human reactions cannot be summed up in any useful way by a set of mathematical relationships. In this contect it is interesting to note that mathematical and statistical model building is now being extended more directly to the general behaviour of human groups and societies in the growing field of mathematical sociology. But the criticism of lack of reality generally speaking misses the point. By definition models are unreal, for their purpose is not to describe reality but to reduce the key features of that reality to more manageable forms for the purpose of decision making and control. The criterion by which we should judge the success or failure of any model-building exercise is the extent to which we have constructed a tool which enables us to achieve our specified objective. Thus, to use a fashionable word, the criterion is pragmatic. In one sense the more realistic is the model the less we have abstracted from the complex process we are trying to control.

Given the definition of a model suggested above it is clear that models that are explicitly referred to as econometric models overlap with a wide class of models that are usually attributable to other workers and researchers who are usually not referred to as econometricians. Thus, for example, classical operational research includes the formulation and study of models of inventory decision and control. Such models require the specification of certain business and economic relations and some statistical treatment of those relations. Econometricians construct empirical demand analyses and operational research workers construct market and marketing models. There is really very little distinction in kind and the labelling of some forms of analysis as econometrics and others as operational research is purely a matter either of convenience or historical accident. There have been historical distinctions in that the econometrician has spent a great deal of his time in dealing with relationships at a fairly high level of aggregation such as the industry level or the level of the economy as a whole. Moreover, most of his effort has been devoted to positive analysis, or the discovery of how the system may be assumed to work, whereas the operational research worker has been concerned with more narrowly defined problems at the level of the individual firm which have been normative in character, i.e. the purpose of the exercises has been to decide what should be done. But even here the distinction is not hard and fast. Again historically there has been the distinction that the bulk of those who carry the econometric flag have had some formal background in economics while the operational research worker has tended to be drawn from mathematics and the physical sciences.

In view of the overlap both in subject matter and method between econometric model building and model building in operational research it is not particularly fruitful to try and uniquely define an econometric model. As pointed out, traditionally the work of econometricians has been related to data and problems at a higher level than that of the individual firm. In particular, as far as complete models are concerned the econometrician has been unique in the attention he has paid to the problem of constructing large scale models of the economy as a whole. In view, therefore, of the wide coverage of this symposium I propose to confine the remainder of this paper to discussing the particular problems of models of this type. Despite this restriction much of the discussion of problems and methodology is widely applicable to complete model systems developed at a lower level of data aggregation.

3 The structure of econometric models

It is convenient, with virtually no loss of generality to discuss the structure of econometric models in terms of the general model that is linear in structural coefficients. This, of course, does not necessarily imply that the model as a whole be treated in linear form, although it is linear in the unknown parameters for estimation purposes. For example, we could measure all the variables in logarithmic form. If some consistency in the form of measurement of variables is not adopted, considerable practical difficulties may arise from the point of view of model solution. Bearing this in mind, we may express the general model in matrix terms as follows :-

$$(1) \quad y = Ay + Bz + u$$

where y is an n by 1 vector of dependent or endogenous variables,

z is a k by 1 vector of independent or exogenous variables and

u is an n by 1 vector of random disturbances with zero mean and finite variances.

It is not generally necessary to specify the probability distribution of u further for the purposes of estimation of the unknown coefficient matrices A and B, beyond some specification of the serial correlation structure. However, the derivation of statistical tests requires detailed specification which means in practice the assumption that the components of u are jointly normally distributed. It may be noted that provided $(I - A)$ is non-singular, we can write (1) in the form :-

$$(2) \quad y = (I - A)^{-1} Bz + (I - A)^{-1} u$$

The definition of the components of the y and z vectors are of crucial importance from a statistical point of view. The components of the y

vector are the endogenous variables that are to be explained or solved
for from the system. The components of the z vector are not explained by
the system, i.e. strictly the elements are distributed independently of the
elements of u. Thus, the system defines the joint distribution of the elements of y given the elements of the vector z. It is of further significance
to partition the vector z into two parts. In the context of time series analysis, some of the elements of z will be lagged values of the elements of
the y vector. Thus, another way of looking at the model defined by (1) is
as a system of linear stochastic difference equations. The time path of
the elements of y are thus determined, in part by changes in the exogenous
factors that are external to the model, in part by the dynamic structure of
the system itself (particularly the coefficient and lag structure) and in part
by the distributed influence of the random perturbations that enter via the
u vector. It must, however, be borne in mind that all structures of this
type are in some sense approximations. Bearing that in mind, it is always
important to recall the distinction between dynamic behaviour in the small
and dynamic behaviour in the large. We shall return to this point later.

The definition of the characteristic of exogenity is in principle easy
but in practice difficult. In analysing economic change we naturally tend
to formulate the structure of the analysis in cause and effect terms. Thus,
at an aggregate level we may say that we expect a rise in consumers'
expenditures on motor cars *because* we expect a rise in consumers' disposable income. But it is clear that what people will spend on motor cars
partly determines what people's incomes are going to be. Now it may be
literally true that income has to be earned before it is spent and so the
cause and effect approach is plausible. But in practice the basic unit time
periods of observation that we use in analysing economic systems are far
longer than some of the inherent lags. Thus, for example, we only measure
the Gross Domestic Product once a quarter and the Index of Industrial
Production once a month. For the typical consumer the income expenditure
lag may often be a week and at most a month except for dividend income.
Thus, the form in which the data appear and are used in a model may
result in simultaneity in the determination of variables. In this case the
cause and effect relation disappears in terms of the model. Thus, we
cannot say that income causes consumption but that income and consumption are jointly dependent variables in the analysis. This issue has
caused some debate among econometricians which we cannot enter into
at length here. A second line of approach is to say that the elements of
the y vector are in some sense caused by the elements of the z vector.
Again strictly the only thing we can say about the elements of the z
vector is that they should be distributed independently of the random disturbances. In many statistical models of the economy as a whole policy
instruments such as tax rates, or the rate of government spending are de-

fined as exogenous to the system. But this is strictly only to fly a flag of convenience or in some cases amounts to an admission of ignorance. Thus, while economic variables, such as output, consumption, investment and employment, may be treated as dependent on certain Government decisions as to tax rates, expenditure and credit conditions, the very values of these policy variables are likely to be dependent on past or expected values of the variables we are trying to explain. Here we would need to introduce some model explaining the formation of Government policy as defined by the vector of values of Government instruments. A recent work by E.T. Balopoulos [2] has considered some of these issues in depth and the interested reader should pursue the subject there.

The structure of a general model like (1) is determined in part by the parameters of the joint probability distribution of the elements of the vector u and in part by the economic structure as represented by the coefficient matrices A and B. Many of the elements of these matrices will be zero, signifying that a particular endogenous or exogenous variable does not appear in a particular equation. The existence of such zeros is at least a necessary condition for the estimation of the parametric structure from economic data, otherwise from a statistical point of view every economic relationship would look exactly like every other. This would be a case of everything depends on everything else with a vengeance, which would leave us without any hope of separating out the effect of one variable on another. Even if the zero non-zero restrictions on these coefficient matrices are such that formally we can separate these effects, there are in fact other practical reasons why this is not always possible.

The elements of the relevant vectors and the coefficient restrictions derive from one's prior theory of how the system behaves. In practice an initial specification of the system is obtained from the application of economic theory and outstanding empirical results. The initial specification is likely itself to be altered as a result of empirical work investigating the nature of the relationships. Characteristically the parameters of the models are estimated from time series data on the variables involved although it is sometimes possible to gain primary or secondary information from survey and budget data or to introduce restrictions on the values of the coefficients based on any special external knowledge. A major difficulty here is that standard economic theory often does not place sufficient restrictions on the empirical results of investigation to enable us to discriminate between hypotheses as clearly as we would like. As an example consider the problem of explaining the investment of producers in fixed plant and equipment. Here there is a wide class of economic theories that state that profits or expected profits provide the basis for business decisions in this area, while there is another class of equally respectable theories that emphasize the level or rate of change of output and future

levels of these variables. Unfortunately in time series the movements in
profits and output are such that it is often not possible to distinguish
clearly between these competing theories. If this cannot be done we are
clearly weakened in our endeavour to assess say the impact of a change
in corporation tax on producers' investment. An analogous problem arises
in trying to explain the deterioration of the UK share of manufactured
exports. There happens to be a fairly high correlation between the decline
of that share and the ratio of the UK export price index to the world price.
But our relative position is declining in other respects, for example, with
respect to our share of world capacity. Such intercorrelations raise knotty
problems for the investigator and lead some to be highly sceptical about
the meaningfulness of some statistically estimated relationships. Healthy
scepticism here is both necessary and important, provided it does not drive
out a legitimate search for knowledge.

It follows from this that the model builder cannot escape a considerable exercise of judgement in constructing and working his model. It
reflects a great deal of his prior knowledge both with respect to the likely
set of hypotheses which he may use to interpret his data and with regard to
the general limitations of his method. It has already been emphasized that
these models are in some sense approximations, and this is reinforced by
the consideration that apart from the formal specification of the variables
that are to enter into his model, he must also specify the precise mathematical forms of the relationships between those variables. Usually he has
no precise idea as to the detailed functional forms except in special cases
where *a priori* considerations may indicate at least some departure from
standard form. For example, in constructing a model of a particular market
process, it may be important to consider the possibility that demand will
become at some point saturated so that the nature of demand will not lead
to any net expansion in the market but merely replacement. In that case it
would be important to specify the non-linear response of demand for that
particular product to increases in purchasing power. The most general
practice, however, is to specify the model in linear or log-linear terms in
either the levels or rates of change of the relevant variables. Thus, variables may enter in non-linear forms such as products or ratios or variables
to a positive or negative power. This reduces the stringency of the linear in
coefficient assumption. Moreover, it is, of course, possible to cite a
general theorem as to the possibility of approximating a non-linear function by a linear one provided that the use of the model remains within
limits set by the degree of the approximation. All this adds up to a demand
for care in asking the model for information that takes it outside its sphere
of usefulness, and for constant reconsideration of the model structure
measured at best against its performance. If model building is to prove of
any lasting value it must be regarded as an activity and not a once and
for all job. It may turn out that the process of revising the working model is

of much greater importance than the initial construction. Indeed one of the problems in this field is the lack of lengthy experience in running major systems. Many models have been constructed and left to stand like the pyramids. Unlike the pyramids their historical interest is soon outweighed by their lack of applicability at a later date.

4. The uses of econometric models

The construction of econometric models serves three main purposes. The first, and by no means the least, is that the construction of such models provides a systematic way of studying the past and specifying the inter-relationships of economic variables that have prevailed over the period for which data is available. Such knowledge does, of course, help to lay a foundation for the second purpose which is the exercise of forecasting or saying something about the future. But the first activity has consider-able importance in its own right and is less demanding in practice as far as information is concerned. The reason for this is that looking back to the general linear model defined by (1) it is clear that in order to project the time path of the jointly dependent variables or elements of the y vector it is necessary to specify in advance the time paths of the elements of the z vector to solve the system for each unit period of time. Now some of these z values will become known in the course of the solution insofar as they are lagged values of the jointly dependent variables. Others, however, will not. Consider this problem in the context of an econometric model that is set up as part of the analysis of the market for a particular commodity. As a concrete example let us take the demand for passenger motor cars as a large well-defined item. Now it is an interesting· and re-vealing exercise to consider what has determined (or what does determine) the demand for motor cars. One important 'explanatory' variable here is the income of consumers, and it is of moment to establish precisely what the relationship between the demand for motor cars and consumers' income is. To the extent that it is believed that this can be established by the con-struction of a suitable model, knowledge is created about the structure of the market. This can be established without any theory of how precisely consumers' income is determined. In forecasting, however, the problem of determining consumers' income cannot be avoided. As further example, it is of some interest to consider the exact character of the American reces-sion in 1949, in particular to establish whether the fluctuation that took place at that time could be described as belonging to the inventory type of cycle. To analyse this problem a model could be set up to simulate the behaviour of the US economy over the relevant period, and it would probably be sensible in doing so to treat US Government expenditures over the period as exogenous to the model, i.e. as part of the z vector. The actual data on this variable could then be introduced into the simulation. When forecasting, however, the actual values of Government spending in the future will not be known and it will be necessary to make some assumptions about them which, of course, may turn out to be incorrect. Thus, the forecast may also turn out to be incorrect, not because the model is itself structurally inappropriate as far as it goes, but because the exogenous information that is fed in is not correct. Thus, it is of some significance to distinguish between the role of the model in telling us something about how a system typically works and the use of the same system to project that system into the future.

The third main purpose of econometric model building is to provide a framework within which to consider policy alternatives. In this case it is convenient to divide the variables that appear in the model into three groups, the jointly dependent variables as before, the elements of the y vector, secondly those elements of the z vector that are exogenous to the model but are not controlled by you, and thirdly those variables that are considered exogenous to the model but over which one exercises control. In·this event the interesting set of relationships are those which define the relation between the dependent variables and the controlled exogenous variables, given some specified set of values of the uncontrolled exogenous variables. For a more detailed consideration of these problems in both Governmental and industrial decision making, reference may be made to Theil [10].

In some respects the first and third of these objectives are in themselves more uniquely associated with the process of explicit model building than the second. For forecasting purposes the classical approach of general time series has much to recommend itself in specific cases. Generally speaking, however, such approaches to forecasting make the use of minimum information, too little to provide any rational basis for policy making that is expected to alter the variable that is being forecast. Thus, it is sometimes said that if forecasting were the sole reason for building elaborate models the cost would outweigh the additional benefit. This contention can itself be debated at length, for the model approach has great flexibility and in many ways permits the more sensible application of judgement and extraneous information. However, as far as model error, i.e. error due to inappropriate structure, is concerned, there is a link between the three purposes, for success in achieving small model errors in forecasting serves in part to validate the use of the model for the other purposes.

It has been emphasised earlier that econometric models must be looked at as tools designed to achieve specific purposes and that judgement exercised on them must be pragmatic. One should perhaps here make the further substantial point, that from another point of view a model can be looked at as a systematic way of organizing information. The structure of the model translates an information input into an information output. Thus, the very activity of model building is itself of value, for in the nature of that activity one undertakes a systematic review of many sources of data that are the elements in a complex decision problem. Thus, the journey itself is often of considerable value, apart from the arrival.

5 Statistical problems of model building

It is perhaps worth commenting briefly at this point on a number of the statistical problems that have been thrown up by econometric model building. Having specified the variables and structural form of the general linear model like (1), it is necessary to estimate the numerical values of the coefficients and other parameters of the structure.

It was said earlier that econometrics is in one sense the meeting point of economic and statistical theory. At one frontier econometrics penetrates into the country of economics and its results figure in the academic journals of the subject. At the other end it is hard to draw any hard and fast line between results that have from a theoretical point of view been established by econometricians and those that have been established by mathematical statisticians. There is in both cases a substantial overlap. There has, however, emerged a class of special statistical problems in which the econometrician has been especially interested which relate to the behaviour of systems of statistical relationships. It was recognised in the 1940's that the estimation of structural coefficients in systems of statistical equations could be satisfactorily treated by traditional multiple correlation analysis in certain special cases. The problem can be seen by inspection of the basic model (1). Classical regression analysis was carried out on the assumption that the variables on the right-hand side of any regression equation were distributed independently of the error or disturbance in that equation. The interpretation of the error was not always made clear but one familiar interpretation was that it reflected an error of measurement in the dependent variable. But since the elements of the y vector, which appear on both the left- and right-side of equations in the system are jointly distributed, the fundamental theory of classical least squares breaks down when account is taken of the system in which the individual relationships are embedded. As a result of recognising this problem, a vast literature has grown up on the problem of estimating structural coefficients in simultaneous systems. For a detailed discussion of some of these methods reference may be made to Johnston [7] and Goldberger [5]. A more non-technical account of the logic of these methods is given in Ball [1].

The existence of systems of relations also raises the difficult problem of identifying the relationships estimated in economic terms. Thus, economic theory may tell us that two economic variables are related together by two patterns of behaviour, e.g. the price of a commodity may affect both the demand for it and the supply, involving both producers' and con-

C

sumers' behaviour. Available data may tell us what has been happening to both the quantity produced and sold and its price, which is the result of the interaction of these two behaviour patterns. Statistical problems now arise in separating out these two behaviour patterns. Sometimes this is not possible in principle and in some other cases it is difficult in practice. This is another special and recurring problem that arises from the existence of a complete set of relationships.

However, even given these sophisticated problems, it remains the case that one of the major problems in practice for the model builder using time series data is that of multicollinearity between the time series used. This is not a formal problem of identification in the sense just discussed, which is formally at least a problem of statistical structure. It is a problem essentially of the sample data, which is a fact of life that usually there is no escape from. This problem in practice is very much greater than those that are treated at great length and with great sophistication in the statistical literature.

6   The solution and behaviour of models

It was pointed out earlier that econometric models can be generally regarded as dynamic systems in that they include as variables lagged values of the dependent variables. Thus, for predetermined time paths of purely exogenous variables, repeated solution of a model will generate the time path of the dependent variables which will in part reflect the relation between the dependent variables and those past values. Insofar as the models are linear in both variables and parameters and the random disturbances are ignored the dynamic properties of such systems can be obtained by the application of standard theory of systems of difference equations. In the past such techniques have often been applied, even where the variables are not generally linear, by replacing non-linear variables by linear approximations and so studying dynamic properties at least in the small, i.e. in the neighbourhood of the approximations. A well known example of this is the study by Goldberger [6].

In recent years, however, such studies have been extended in two ways. Firstly, as pointed out, the dynamic properties of systems have been studied neglecting the disturbance terms by setting them equal to zero. When this has been done it is usually found that the resulting systems contain endogenous dynamic mechanisms that are inherently stable. At one level this is an important finding where the model in question is related to underlying data that exhibit a cyclical pattern, e.g. as in the case of the Gross Domestic Product in the US. Business cycle theorists have long debated the issue as to whether the cycles that occur are endogenous to the economic system in the sense that the underlying behavioural structure generates a continuous fluctuation unless countered by explicit policy action to prevent it. An alternative class of theories argues that the underlying behavioural mechanism is in fact stable, but is constantly disturbed by shocks and perturbations imposed from outside the system, some of which may be purely random. There are a variety of these shock theories of business fluctuations. Some studies have shown that where the random components of relations are concerned, their reintroduction into the solution process by a simulation procedure results in the models generating cyclical paths of the appropriate period and amplitude that correspond to the cycles observed in the basic data. From these results some have concluded that the shock models of the cycles come nearest to the truth. This conclusion is in fact open to considerable debate which we cannot pursue here. But developments of this kind reflect the increasing use of simulation techniques in studying the overall behaviour of econometric models. The second and obvious natural extension of this process is the development of better computer programs for handling these systems, which will do away with the necessity of having to linearize all the variables. Various methods are now available and programmed for iterative solutions that enable models to be handled and simulated quite generally without the restrictions that have been imposed hitherto. These are fairly recent developments and further results of the application of simulations of this type are to be expected.

7 History and assessment of models

The development of the electronic computer has been a key factor in the growth of research into econometric model building. In the absence of the computer the efficient and flexible handling of systems of relations even as small as 20 relations presents a major problem. Thus, up to ten years ago, while a number of economy wide models had been built, comparatively little analysis had been done on their properties and the way in which they might be used. Even now there is a great deal of research to do and much to learn about the behaviour of systems. Ten years ago work on economy wide models had been carried out in the US under the auspices for the most part of Lawrence Klein, and in Holland following in the tradition begun by the pioneer of economic statistical model building, Jan Tinbergen. As of now such economy wide models have been constructed and used for many countries of the world including Japan (where a great deal has now been done) Israel, Greece, Norway, Sweden, Canada, and the United Kingdom. The early work carried out by Klein and others on UK data (8) was largely abortive, as the nature of the data used at the time did not encourage the development and extension of that model. More recently the development of quarterly national income accounts for the UK have encouraged the current research work that is being undertaken at the London Business School.

In view of the lack of development work that has been carried out in the past, we have not yet reached a stage where the costs and benefits of econometric model building can be adequately assessed, although the recent work carried out by Klein and his associates in the US is bringing us nearer that goal. Four years ago when writing on this subject, I expressed the view that the forecasting result of economy wide econometric models had been disappointing, but added that such results could not be held to judge the approach adequately in view of the lack of development work undertaken. At that time there was little evidence based on the development of a model over time, with perhaps the exception of the report based on an annual model given by Daniel Suits [9]. Here the results were extremely interesting and clearly reflected the learning process that is inherent in model building. Again one cannot emphasize enough that model building is a continuous activity with a significant learning process that goes on after a model is constructed and begun to be used. An analogy can be drawn here between the development of statistical models and the development of aircraft. The first stage is the development of the prototype which must then be tested against the performance. Once the unit is put together, there is no guarantee that it will perform effectively. A continual process of modification is necessary against actual experience with the hope that ultimately one will iterate to something useful.

As facilities for handling larger models have become available, there has been some tendency to consider models of increasingly large size. The major example of this is the SSRC-Brookings model, developed by a substantial team of econometricians in the US, which is described in [3]. In its full form this model of the US economy runs to something between 300 and 400 relations. Size in itself is of course no virtue and the increase in system size brings with it both intellectual and organizational problems. It is a major activity to establish the behaviour of systems of this size, and in particular to discover where the system goes wrong. There are also considerable problems of system evaluation, for it cannot be decided how good your system is without specifying your objective. Typically, in large systems, some variables are predicted or simulated well and others badly. Some dispute has arisen over this question and it is worth considering in this context the contribution by Friend and Jones [4] and the ensuing discussion.

A further likely and in part ongoing development is the growth of fully articulated forecasting and control systems that move down from the economy to the industry and thence to the firm level. It is a more typical practice of large American corporations to develop their sales budgeting systems in a fully articulated way, beginning with a view or model of the economy as a whole, rather than developing industry, division and product assessments on a fully coherent basis. Such developments can be run concurrently with grass roots forecasts, i.e. those sometimes used in budgeting which start from the ground up from the direct assessments of sales managers and salesmen in touch with the market. Such fully articulated systems require increased knowledge of the inter-industry structure and it is here that the typical econometric model-building approach joins hands with the techniques of input output analysis.

One can anticipate that research into the development and performance of statistical systems will continue to expand. The growth in information about general economic and market variables and the growth of systems of analysis and data processing all demand conceptual frameworks and quantitative frameworks within which this data can be handled. The econometrician seeks to develop such frameworks in terms of both submodels and complete systems of relationships. Such developments can never eliminate the judgement and experience of the model builder resulting in some completely computerized operation. In forecasting, for example, the model is a tool that assists the forecaster in reaching a forecast. It provides a system for processing and jointly considering the interaction of a variety of information. There is no loss of flexibility in this process, indeed the process itself is an attempt to control the inflow of information in reaching decisions. By the probabilistic nature of the structure of that process the decision will not always be correct. But the model-building approach provides an avenue to a more scientific consideration of information flows and hence more rational decision making.

References

[1] R.J. Ball, 'The Logic of Simultaneous Estimation', *Applied Statistics*, 1963.

[2] E.T. Balopoulos, *Fiscal Policy Models of the British Economy*, North Holland Publishing Company, 1967.

[3] J.S. Duesenberry, G. Fromm, L.R. Klein and E. Kuh (editors) *The Brookings Quarterly Econometric Model of the United States*, North Holland Publishing Company, 1965.

[4] I. Friend and R.C. Jones, 'Short-run Forecasting Models Incorporating Anticipatory Data', from *Models of Income Determination*, by the Conference on Research in Income and Wealth, Princeton University Press, 1964.

[5] A.S. Goldberger, *Econometric Theory*, John Wiley & Sons, Inc., 1964.

[6] A.S. Goldberger, *Impact Multipliers and Dynamic Properties of the Klein-Goldberger Model*, North Holland Publishing Company, 1959.

[7] J. Johnston, *Econometric Methods*, McGraw-Hill Book Company, Inc., 1963.

[8] L.R. Klein, R.J. Ball, A. Hazelwood and P. Vandome, *An Econometric Model of the United Kingdom*, Basil Blackwell & Sons, 1961.

[9] D. Suits, 'Forecasting with an Econometric Model', *American Economic Review*, March 1962.

[10] H. Theil, *Decision Rules for Government & Industry*, North Holland Publishing Company, 1964.

AN EXPERIMENTAL MEDIUM-TERM
MACRO MODEL FOR THE DUTCH ECONOMY

C. A. VAN DEN BELD

1

The Dutch government deals, of course, with both short-term and long-term problems. It is characteristic, however, that until recently the short-term problems have been approached in a far more systematic way than the longer-term ones.

The short-term policy is largely a policy of stabilization. Its main feature is that the actions in this field are fitted each year into the framework of a short-term projection giving a consistent account of economic developments in the coming year. Such projections are published annually by the Dutch Central Planning Bureau in the form of a so called Central Economic Plan. These plans, which are macro economic forecasts rather than plans in the narrow sense of the word, indicate the lines of the government's policy, in particular as the econometric model technique of forecasting makes it possible to present alternative forecasts under alternative policy assumptions. The annual forecasts have some bearing, too, on the process of wage formation, which is at present largely but not fully beyond government control. In addition, a number of firms make use of the macro predictions when they prepare their own annual projections.

Central Economic Plans have been published ever since 1947, and they are now an indispensible part of the economic policy machinery of the central government.

This is not to say that longer-term developments were completely ignored. There are indeed several examples of medium or long-term analyses. However, for a long time the approach in this field was of an incidental character and certainly less systematic than in the case of the annual plans.

This situation has changed in recent years, when the government began to lay more emphasis on growth and other aspects of long-term development. More specifically, it announced in 1963 that it would attach particular importance to the analysis of medium-term perspectives. This led to a program of action in 1964, which included medium-term projections to be set up for the economy as a whole as well as for a number of individual branches of industry, the latter to be made in co-operation with the industries themselves.

This shift in emphasis cannot be seen independently of the fact that several groupings, among them trade unions and employer's organizations, felt it more and more desirable to combine the analysis of the annual plans with a longer-run perspective. In addition, the problems of growing international co-operation called for such projections.

The first result of the governmental initiative was *The Dutch Economy in 1970*, a recent publication by the Central Planning Bureau [1]. This study describes the economic situation in 1970, in macro terms as well as for a number of branches of industry. The projections were made in close co-operation with experts from some industrial sectors. But, the now already long tradition of model building in the Netherlands was maintained. Again, therefore, it proved to be possible to present alternative forecasts under alternative policy assumptions, thus showing the impact of government actions on medium-term developments.

Since the system of medium-term planning is envisaged to be a revolving one, the first publication will be followed — though not annually — by others in which projections made earlier will be revised and extended beyond 1970.

2

The precedent for building *short-term* models was set as early as 1936, when Tinbergen constructed a system of simultaneous equations to predict the macro effects of the devaluation of the Dutch guilder in that year. After 1945 the Tinbergen tradition was carried on by the Central Planning Bureau.

Up until 1958 the short-term models were linear and mainly static. Later models, however, are non-linear and highly dynamic, as can be seen if the model published in the Central Economic Plan for 1955 is compared with the one published in 1961. In addition, use had been made in later models of more refined methods of parameter estimation. But, both the older and the newer short-term models are macro- economic, describing annual movements of the economy, and constructed for purposes of prediction as well as the calculation of policy alternatives.

The present short-term model — which is of 1963 — consists of thirty-eight equations, among them thirteen reaction equations most of which have been estimated by means of the limited-information maximum-likelihood method, the others on the basis of two-stage least squares. The sampling period covers the years 1923-1938 and 1949-1960. The greater part of the variables is expressed in relative first differences, which device not only reduces multicollinearity but also facilitates the estimation of time lags.

[1] *De Nederlandse Economie in 1970*, Central Planning Bureau, 1966. An English version of this publication is in preparation.

The 1963 model is to a large extent a demand model. Four of the thirteen reaction equations are demand equations for expenditure categories, two others represent the demand for factors of production, *viz.* imports and labour. A production function is lacking. The supply side nevertheless is included in the model via five price equations as well as a capacity factor, the latter represented by the level of labour unemployment. The capacity variable plays a central non-linear role in the system. It appears in six of the thirteen reaction equations [1]. A monetary variable appears in four equations, its impact being largest on investment demand. Like labour unemployment, liquidities are treated endogenously, mainly as a function of the balance of payments current account.

The present *medium-term* model — which is of 1966 — has been designed for the purpose of projecting medium-term sectoral and macro developments. The model includes twenty three branches of industry and refers to 1970 as year of projection, 1965 being chosen as base-year [2]. Developments between these two bench-mark years are assumed to be characterized by constant rates of growth. The model is a closed system. The totals of final demand, therefore, are not obtained from some macro analysis, but follow endogenously from the model. Other features are the introduction of production functions and price levels by sector, the interaction between volumes and prices, and the use of marginal rather than average values of the technical coefficients. Characteristic, too, are some macro relations. Total private consumption, for example, is a function of total disposable wage and non-wage income respectively. The wage relation also is in the first instance macro. It is in this way that the traditional policy variables of the short-term analysis are entered in the medium-term system. Furthermore, an assumption has been introduced concerning the desired balance of payment surplus in the year of projection.

By distinguishing twenty three sectors the model has become very large, the number of equations being over three hundred. To facilitate the solution of the model all the relationships are supposed to be linear, originally non-linear relations having been linearized around the *expected* 1970 values. The sampling period covers post-war years only. The methods of parameters estimation were far from sophisticated; ordinary least-squares and graphical inspection prevailed, while in a number of cases coefficients had to be chosen on a more or less *a priori* basis.

---

[1] Cf. P. J. Verdoorn and J. J. Post 'Capacity and short-term multipliers', in: Hart, Mills and Whitaker: Econometric analysis for national economic planning (Colston papers No. 16, London 1964).

[2] This model will be published in the English version of *The Dutch Economy in 1970* referred to above.

3

Leaving aside — for reasons which will become clear below — the specific branches of industry results obtained from the medium-term model, we may conclude that its macro outcomes are comparable with those of the short-term model in so far as:

- both models predict volumes as well as prices, and
- both contain largely the same set of exogenous and endogenous variables, among them government-controlled and non-controlled ones.

The position that has been reached in this way is nevertheless not wholly satisfactory. The short-term model is highly dynamic, but it does not explain capacity output. The medium-term analysis does explain capacity, but it is static in the sense that it projects one and only one year, while assuming a constant rate of growth over time. The obvious and important problem which remains is the fact of life that cycles and growth go together. This point was already very clearly discussed by Arthur Smithies in 1957 in his 'Economic Fluctuations and Growth' [1], where he states that:

'The last twenty five years have seen a wealth of business-cycle theories which attempt to explain fluctuations about a growth trend, but leave the trend itself largely unexplained. (On the other hand, he says) many of the dynamic theories of the post-war period have been preoccupied with the conditions for steady growth and have neglected what happens when the economy leaves its narrow exponential path. Bridges between these two types of theory are infrequent and by no means satisfactory.'

Smithies constructs what may be called a model of cyclical growth. His model is empirical in the sense that the possibilities it suggests are not excluded by available evidence. But it is not numerical. In fact, Smithies doubts whether satisfactory numerical models can be constructed as long as we have to rely heavily on the evidence of time series.

The present author does not want to go as far as this. On the contrary, what seems to be highly desirable at the present stage of Dutch model building is to construct a model of cyclical growth in numerical terms, thus arriving at some integration of the existing short- and medium-term systems.

It is the purpose of this note to introduce such a model and to try it out. That model is, as will be seen, a purely macro one. It does not distinguish between (large) sectors of the economy, which is perhaps the

---

[1] *Econometrica*, January 1957.

most serious limitation on the way towards the construction of what may be considered an ideal model. Since it combines Cyclical and Structural elements, the model presented below will be referred to as a CS-model. Its main structure is discussed in some detail in the next section.

4

The reaction equations of the CS-model are given on pages 35 to 37. All the equations are on an annual basis. The system thus describes the time path of development from one year to another.

The total number of reaction equations is twenty one [1]. In general, the variables refer to levels; variables with a dot, however, represent percentage changes (divided by 100). Unless otherwise indicated, capital symbols refer to values, small symbols to volumes or prices. The exogenous variables of the system are underlined.

CS-model [2]

I. Productive capacity, production and surplus capacity

1. $\Delta c_a = a_{t_{-1}} \underline{\Delta a^*_b} + 0.275 i_{-1} + \underline{\Delta c^*_a}$

2. $y_b = c + c_g + i + i_g + \underline{i_{cg}} + \Delta n + b_m + \underline{b_s} - m_m - \underline{g} - \underline{d_g}$

3. $q = (c_a - y_b)/c_{a_{-1}}$

II. Labour demand and supply

4. $\Delta P = -0.500 \, (\Delta w + \Delta w_{-1}) + \underline{\Delta P_D}$

5. $\dot{a}_b = 0.304 \dot{y}'_b + 0.158 \dot{y}'_{b_{-1}} - 0.013$

III. Domestic expenditure and stock formation

6. $C = 1.000 \, L^D + 0.125 \, (Z^D + Z^D_{-1}) + 4.400 \dot{p}_c -$

   $-43.000 r_{-1} + 4.780 \text{ (if } r_{-1} \geqslant 0.040$

7. $i = 0.167 v_{-1} + 0.852 \dfrac{0.100}{q_{-1} + 0.080} + 27.500 \left[\dfrac{L_q}{Y}\right]_{-1} +$

   $+ \underline{i^*} - 14.730 \text{ (if } \left[\dfrac{L_q}{Y}\right]_{-1} \leqslant 0.43)$

---

[1] There are twenty four equations on pages 35 to 37, but three of them are definitions. The equations (2) and (3) define GNP and surplus capacity

8. $\Delta n = 0.331\,\Delta v - 9.970\,\Delta(\Delta v/v_{-1}) + \underline{\Delta n_v} - 0.249$

9. $i_g = -13.750 r_{-1} + \underline{i^*{}_g}$

IV. Merchandise imports and exports

10. $m_m = 0.455 v + 0.842\,\Delta_n - 0.832\,\underline{y_a} + \underline{m^*{}_m} - 3.519$

11. $b_m = 1.007\,\underline{m_w} + 0.162\,\displaystyle\sum_0^t K_{-1} - \dfrac{2.607}{q'_{-1} + 2} + 1.291$

V. Wage level, rate of interest and prices

12. $l = 0.220\,(\dot p_c + \dot p_{c_{-1}} + \dot p_{c_{-2}}) + 0.400\,(\dot h + \dot h_{-1}) -$

$\qquad - 0.045\,(w + w_{-1}) + 0.086$

13. $r = \left[\dfrac{0.001}{\dfrac{L_q}{Y} - 0.350}\right] - 0.020\,(\Delta i/i_{-1} + \Delta i_{-1}/i_{-2}) + 0.027$

14. $\dot p'_c = 0.250\,(l + l_{-1}) - 0.250\,(\dot h + \dot h_{-1}) + 0.250\,\underline{\dot p_{mr}} -$

$\qquad - 1.000\,\Delta(n'/v)_{-1} + 0.006$

15. $\dot p_{cg} = 0.500\,(l - \dot h_{-\frac12}) + 0.300\,\underline{\dot p_m} - 0.437\,(q + q_{-1}) -$

$\qquad - 0.013 t + 0.012\ (\text{if } \dfrac{q + q_{-1}}{2} \leqslant 0.02)$

16. $\dot p'_i = 0.250\,(l - \dot h_{-\frac12}) + 0.300\,\underline{\dot p_{mr}} - 1.250\,q + 0.030$

$\qquad (\text{if } q \leqslant 0.02)$

17. $\dot p_{i_g} = 0.500\,(l - \dot h_{-\frac12}) + 0.300\,\underline{\dot p_m} - 0.475\,(q + q_{-1}) + 0.042$

18. $\dot p_{i_{cg}} = 0.300\,\left\{(l - \dot h_{-\frac12}) + (l - \dot h_{-\frac12})_{-1}\right\} + 0.300\,\underline{\dot p_m} -$

$\qquad - 0.500\,(q + q_{-1})\ (\text{if } \dfrac{q + q_{-1}}{2} \leqslant 0.02)$

(continued from previous page)
respectively, while equation (24) is a definition of money creation via
external payments.

[2] Underlined variables are exogenous. Symbols, notation and choice of units are
explained in the appendix.

VI. Taxes

19. $\Delta T_L = 0.199 \Delta L^Z + 3.500 (T_L/L^Z)_{-1} + \underline{\Delta T^*_L} - 0.377$

20. $\Delta T_K = 0.110 \Delta V_D + \underline{\Delta T^*_K}$

21. $\Delta T_Z = 0.400 \Delta Z^Z + \underline{\Delta T^*_Z}$

VII. Creation of liquidities

22. $\Delta L_{q(ba)} = 0.185 \Delta Y - 6.600 \Delta q - 29.000 \underline{\Delta r'} + \underline{\Delta L^*_{q(ba)}}$

23. $\Delta L_{q(g)} = -0.595 \Delta L_{q(ex)} + 24.700 \dfrac{w}{P_B} - 14.072 \left(\dfrac{L_q}{Y}\right)_{-1} +$

$+ \underline{\Delta L^*_{q(g)}} + 5.900$

24. $\Delta L_{q(ex)} = (B - M) + \underline{\Delta L^*_{q(ex)}}$

The sampling period covers post-war years only. The structural coefficients were estimated on the basis of simple least-squares. Advanced methods of parameter estimation were not used in the present stage which is still experimental, mainly because some of the specifications certainly have to be improved. In a number of cases, notably the price equations, multicollinearity led to unreliable results. Under such circumstances the values of the coefficients — including the time-lags involved — were borrowed from the short-term model. A further complication arises from non-lagged curvilinearities in the system. Graphical inspection shows, however, that these curvilinearities can be approximated fairly well by two (and only two) straight-line relationships. This explains why some of the reaction equations are indicated to hold within a certain interval. For example, the linear price equation (15) is indicated to be valid as long as surplus capacity does not exceed 2 per cent; if it exceeds this percentage, equation (15) has to be replaced by another one in which the capacity variable in fact does not enter at all [1].

In summary, parameter estimation was based on simple least-squares, on information provided by the existing short-term model as well as on free-hand linear approximation of curvilinearities.

---

[1] In order to simplify the presentation of the model this relation is not shown.

The first set of equations on page 35 refers to capacity output and actual production. Capacity output is assumed to be generated by additional labour and gross investment, where the marginal contribution of labour has been assumed to be equal to the level of real wages. Autonomous changes in capacity, caused e.g. by changes in weather conditions and working hours, are taken into account separately (1). [1].

Surplus capacity is defined in terms of potential and actual production (3), which stands in major contrast with the existing short-term model where it is defined in terms of labour unemployment (cf. above).

There follow two equations for labour demand and supply respectively. The latter is largely determined by demographical factors, but is partly endogenous since participation rates tend to vary with the labour market situation (4). Labour demand (5) is a function of GNP only. The specification of this relation certainly has to be improved in order to account for substitution between labour and capital.

Private consumption, in the third group of equations, has disposable wage and non-wage income as its main determinants. This is a relation in value terms (6). Business investment in fixed assests, on the other hand, is a volume equation (7). This type of investment appears to be non-linear in the capacity as well as in the monetary variable. Stock formation (8) stands in simple relation to the volume of total sales, but there is some involuntary accumulation of stocks when the rise in demand is slow (and vice versa).

Housing plus investment by local authorities (9) is largely considered as exogenous, but partly dependent on the situation on the capital market, represented by the long-term rate of interest.

The fourth set of equations refers to merchandise imports and exports. In the imports equation (10) the volume of total sales is the decisive variable; in addition to this, the high import content in stock formation has to be taken into account. Autonomous changes in imports arise from changes in agricultural output at home as well as from changes in tariffs.

The main determinant of exports is the volume of world trade, but surplus capacity at home also plays an important, non-linear, role. Thirdly, the growth of exports is seen as a function of unit-labour cost levels relative to those of competitors abroad. In this way the fundamental competitive position of the Dutch economy appears in the system.

The price equations (14 to 18) are of the usual type, since prices of expenditure are explained in terms of import prices, wage level and labour productivity. In addition, prices are non-linear in the capacity variable; consumption prices, however, seem to be influenced by stock positions

---

[1] Numbers between parentheses in this section refer to the numbers of the equations.

rather than capacity. There is no price equation for exports, because of the close correspondence between export prices and competitive prices abroad during the sampling period.

The variables appearing in the wage level equation (12) are the traditional ones: labour productivity, consumption prices and labour unemployment. Less traditional perhaps is the explanation of the rate of interest (13), which is not only non-linear in available monetary reserves but also negatively correlated with the rate of increase in investment. This seems to indicate that liquidity preferences vary with the phase of the cycle.

Three tax equations (19 to 21) appear in the system in order to arrive at disposable wage and non-wage income. For that purpose taxes are distinguished between indirect taxes and direct taxes on wage and non-wage income respectively.

Finally, the system has to explain money creation (including near-money), because of the appearance of monetary variables in some of the domestic expenditure equations. Money is seen as being created by the banking system, by the government and via external payments (22 to 24). The latter is endogenous in so far as it results from the balance of payments current account. Even money creation by the government is seen as endogenous, depending *inter alia* on the balance of payments and the labour market situation. This point will be discussed at some length below.

5

It seems useful to summarize the above by considering the general line of thought which underlies the model.

The model explains the growth of the economy by exogenous factors on the demand side, viz.

— the volume of world trade, and
— autonomous components of demand, like investment in housing and government expenditure.

Supply factors, however, are equally important. For the rise in exports also depends on available capacity and the relative level of costs (11).

If it is assumed that the rise in exports as well as in autonomous demand is strong, the demand for investment by the business sector tends to accelerate, not only because of the higher level of sales but also as a consequence of a larger influx of liquidities from abroad (7, 24). The volume expansion then gathers momentum since unemployment falls, which causes a strong upward movement in wages and private consumption (12, 6). This process of volume expansion may continue until capacity limits are reached. The result then is a strong upward pressure on prices and wages. In addition, the volume of exports will be adversely affected (11). The ensuing deficit on the balance of payments current account leads to an outflow of liquidities, which causes monetary tensions. The latter may be mitigated by inflationary financing by the government (23). If, however, monetary tensions remain strong, business investment and other components of domestic demand will be affected (6, 7, 9), thus causing a stagnation in production as well as a rise in unemployment, Under these circumstances, the phase of true price inflation is followed by a recession, characterized by low increases in wages and prices. The length and the intensity of the recession depend on the fundamental competitive position of the economy as well as on new shocks to which the economy may be subject (world trade, autonomous domestic expenditure).

The above is, in a very few words, the line of reasoning underlying the model. It shows how the economy may fluctuate as a consequence of internal and/or external shocks. Essential elements in this process are the mechanism of multiplier and flexible accelerator, the exhaustion of capacity, the aggravation of price inflation, and finally the depletion of monetary reserves. The long-term growth of capacity output results mainly from the cumulative amount of gross investment.

Of course, the present analysis is to a large extent analogous to the approach followed in the existing short-term model. Differences arise, however, from the introduction of the capacity-creating aspect of invest-ment as well as from the fundamental competitive position of the economy. Furthermore, the model presented here integrates more fully what are usually called the real and the monetary spheres. Finally, the present model tries to describe government behaviour, mainly in the monetary field. This may seen strange at first sight. But, if the model is tried out, the assumption of an autonomous monetary policy would be highly unreal-istic.

6

Since it is the purpose of the CS-model to predict economic development over a number of consecutive years, two specific conditions have to be fulfilled as to the construction of the model and its programming on the computer :

(i) the model must be phased, that is, it should contain dynamic definition equations which logically connect one phase (year) to another. For example, if the model predicts the amount of money creation in some year, it should add this up to the initial total amount of money in circulation in order to arrive at the new initial level for the next period.

(ii) in the case of linear approximation of non-lagged curvilinearities,

programming should be such as to let the computer choose that
linear approximation which is relevant in the predic*ed situation.

If these two conditions are fulfilled [1], the model undoubtedly offers
a very wide perspective for experiments. Thus far, however, only one experiment has been carried out. It has been studied whether the model can
indeed predict actual developments over a number of years in the recent
past.

For this purpose 1953 was chosen as initial situation. On that basis
a prediction was made of 1954, taking exogenous variables like world
trade and world market prices as exactly known. It is this — conditional —
prediction of 1954 which is then the basis for the 1955 prediction, which
is again conditional, since it presupposes again perfect knowledge of the
exogenous data. In this way the experiment has been carried on, up until
the year 1963. The experiment, therefore, involves ten conditional predictions, which is the greater part of the sampling period and twice as
long as the normal medium-term projection period.

Actual developments in these years were characterized by growth and
cyclical fluctuations:

- 1953 shows an upturn in investment (after some recession in 1952)
  as well as a considerable rise in exports, the latter partly as a
  consequence of a very favourable competitive position on international markets;
- in 1954 and 1955 the volume expansion of internal and external
  demand gathers momentum;
- 1956 shows bottle-necks in production resulting in a balance-of-
  payments deficit; wage increases are then high since unemployment is low; monetary reserves are depleted;
- 1957 is a year of true price inflation, followed by a stagnation in
  internal demand; business investment in particular falls considerably in 1958, but exports develop rather favourably, because of
  capacity surpluses at home and price competitiveness abroad;
- the light recession of 1958 is followed by an upturn in investment
  already in 1959;
- in 1960 the expansion of internal and external demand gathers
  momentum again;
- the years 1962 and 1963 show a further expansion of the economy,
  in terms of volumes and prices, after a reduction of working hours
  as well as a currency revaluation in 1961.

---

[1] The author wants to express his thanks to Messrs. Neeteson, van de Pas, and
Tjan of the Central Planning Bureau for their invaluable help in this and other
programming aspects.

D

Thus, the period 1953 to 1963 covers a full cycle from 1953 up until 1959, followed by a phase of continued expansion afterwards.

It is certainly doubtful whether the model can predict such a development of cyclical growth, notwithstanding the coincidence of experimental and sampling period. For the standard of predictive accuracy imposed upon the model is very high, much higher than in a short-term model where each base year is considered as exactly known. To formulate this in more technical terms: in a short-term model the lagged endogenous variables are predetermined; in a phased model, however, they remain endogenous. In more practical terms: the model prediction of e.g. 1963 in the present experiment does not only depend on the predetermined situation of 1962, but on all the model predictions from 1954 onwards, given the initial situation of 1953. It goes without saying that in such an experiment, errors made in the prediction of one year may cumulate in the predictions of subsequent years, thus leading to a forecast which is far from reality. That is the very reason for the experiment.

The first test proved to be unsuccessful. In fact, the model predicted too small a recession in 1958. Some adjustments were necessary, mainly in the monetary variables and their non-linear impact on domestic expenditure. This seemed to stress the importance of the monetary element in actual developments. A more successful result could be obtained, after a small number of trials only. As the model stands now, it fairly-well predicts not only the growth of the economy but also its fluctuation in investments, unemployment and the balance of payments current account. On the other hand, there is also some cumulation in errors — a point already referred to above. In particular, price levels are over-estimated in the second half of the period. This is shown in graph 1. The graph makes it also clear that the over-estimation of price levels is to be explained mainly by a forecasting error in the level of unemployment in only one year, viz. 1957, which error does not disappear in subsequent years.

The experiment has been closed with an inquiry into the quality of the C S-model predictions. Comparing predicted percentage changes from year to year with those realized, the following measure of predictive accuracy may be used

$$U'_{i,t} = \frac{U_{i,t}}{S_{R_i}}$$

Here $U_{i,t} = F_{i,t} - R_{i,t}$ that is, the forecast minus the realized percentage change in variable i at time t. S_{R_i} denotes the root-mean-square of the observed percentage changes in variable i, taken from zero. This statistic is meant to represent the normal intensity of change of

GRAPH 1 — MODEL PREDICTION AND REALIZATION
1954 - 1963

43

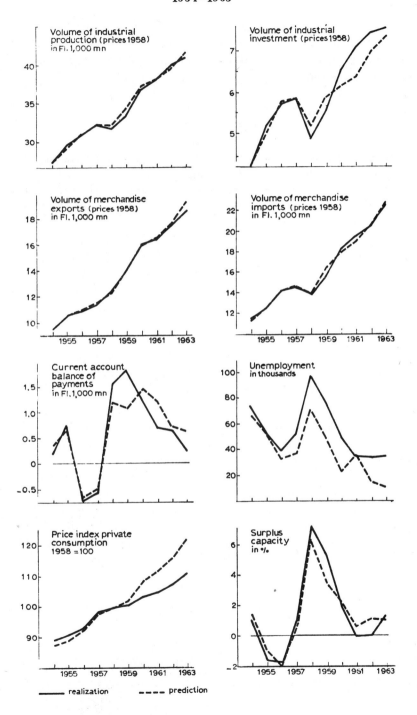

realization   ---- prediction

variable i during the period of observation.

This standardization of errors has the advantage of making them comparable between different variables; moreover, it allows a simple aggregation of the errors of several variables by periods. Accordingly, the following overall inequality coefficient is obtained

$$\bar{U}^1 = \left\{ \frac{1}{mn} \sum_{i=1}^{m} \sum_{t=1}^{n} \bar{U}^{1\,2}_{i,t} \right\}^{\frac{1}{2}}$$

This coefficient has also been used to test the predictive power of the existing short-term model [1]. Its interpretation is simple. The inequality coefficient is zero in the case of perfect prediction; it equals unity if the forecasting errors are as large as the normal rates of change of the variables concerned.

The experiment with the C S-model shows the following inequality coefficients:

Year	Coeff.	Year	Coeff.
1954	0·29	1959	0·45
55	0·22	60	0·58
56	0·23	61	0·43
57	0·23	62	0·36
58	0·33	63	0·35

The predictive accuracy of the existing 1963 short-term model is characterized by an inequality coefficient of about 0.30. The predictive accuracy of the C S-model in the experiment may thus be considered as satisfactory, the more so because the standard of accuracy imposed on the C S-model is higher than that imposed on a short-term model (cf. above).

The foregoing is not the whole story of the predictive power of the C S-model. That power should also be judged in terms of predicted levels instead of year-to-year changes in the variables. Such calculations, however, have not been made, since there is no basis of comparison.

7

The construction of a C S-model may be seen as an obvious step at the present stage of Dutch model building. Equally obvious are further

---

[1] Cf. 'Forecasts and realization', *The forecasts by the Central Planning Bureau, 1953-1963, monograph no. 10,* 1965.

experiments with the C S-model. Such experiments should include predictions of future as well as past developments under different policy assumptions. There is no doubt that such experiments can contribute substantially to an improvement of the present short- and medium-term regulation of the economy.

APPENDIX

List of symbols
(in alphabetical order)

Symbol	Description
a_b	employment in industries
a^*_b	labour supply available for industries
B	total exports
b_s	net exports of services
b_m	merchandise exports
C,c	private consumption
$c_a(*)$	(autonomous) [1] productive capacity
c_g	government consumption expenditure, excluding wages and salaries
d_g	government depreciation allowances
g	government contribution to gross national product (imputed interest only)
h	labour productivity in industries
i	gross industrial investment in fixed assets, excluding housing
i^*	gross investment in aircraft and ships
$i_g(*)$	(autonomous) gross investment expenditure by local authorities plus investment in housing
i_{cg}	gross investment expenditure by central government
K	advantage in labour costs over foreign competitors
l	wage level in industries
L_q	total amount of liquidities in circulation

[1] Autonomous changes in productive capacity result from changes in weather conditions, working hours etc.

Symbol	Description
$\Delta L_{q(ba)}(*)$	(autonomous) creation of liquidities by banks
$\Delta L_{q(g)}(*)$	(autonomous) creation of liquidities by the government
$\Delta L_{q(ex)}(*)$	(autonomous) creation of liquidities via external payments
L^D	disposable wage income
L^Z	taxable wage income
M	total imports
$m_m(*)$	(autonomous) merchandise imports
m_w	reweighted [1] world imports
n	goods in stock
n'	do., excluding live stock
n_v	live stock
p_c	price level of private consumption
p_c'	do., excluding consumption goods imported
p_{cg}	price level of government consumption
p_i'	price level of industrial investment, excluding investment goods imported
$p_{i_{cg}}$	price level of central government investment
p_{i_g}	price level of local government investment plus investment in housing
p_{mr}	price level of raw materials imported
p_m	price level of total imports
P	labour supply
P_D	labour supply as it is being determined by demographic factors, including external migration of labour
P_B	dependent working population
q	surplus capacity
q'	do., in 1 000 mln guilders

[1] Reweighted on the basis of the geographical distribution of Dutch exports.

Symbol	Description
r	rate of interest
r'	official discount rate
t	trend factor
$T_L(*)$	(autonomous) taxes on wage income
$T_K(*)$	(autonomous) indirect taxes minus subsidies
$T_Z(*)$	(autonomous) taxes on non wage income
v	total sales, excluding invisible exports and stock formation
V_D	total sales, excluding exports of goods and services, including stock formation
w	unemployment
y_b	gross national product in industries, at market prices
y_b'	do., adjusted for weather influences
y_a	agricultural production
Y_D	gross national product, at market prices
Z^D	disposable non-wage income
Z^Z	taxable non-wage income
α	marginal contribution of labour to productive capacity

Notation and choice of units

Unless otherwise indicated the variables in the model refer to levels. In general, capital symbols refer to values in current prices, small symbols to volumes in constant prices of 1958 (1 000 mln guilders). Variables on population and unemployment are in numbers ($\times$ 100 000). Variables with a dot refer to percentage changes (: 100).

Underlined variables are exogenous.

ECONOMIC AND SOCIAL MODELLING

J. R. N. STONE

1 Introduction

Professor Ball told us this morning that econometrics was about thirty years old and that economic model building began in the 1930's. It might be of some interest to ask why it did not begin a good deal earlier. The second half of the nineteenth century saw in the field of mathematical economics a tremendous clarification of ideas about the general relationships governing economic life, and it is at first sight surprising that many of the great names associated with that movement did not try their hand at empirical model building. It might be answered that perhaps the most important reason why this did not happen until something between a generation and two generations later was that the climate of opinion was not favourable: that on the whole at that time people were satisfied with the economic, if not with the social, aspects of society; that they were quite happy with their competitive free enterprise system; and that therefore they did not see any great point in building economic models, the main purpose of which, I suppose, is to understand better how the economy works because one is not very satisfied with the way it is working and one would like to improve it. But we have only got to move into the early years of the twentieth century, at any rate in this country, to see that people were not in fact satisfied with the way the economy was working. So I think we shall have to look a bit further than just the climate of opinion — though doubtless this is important — to find out why it took econometrics so long to follow up the great classical systematizing.

I think there are a number of factors which made it difficult at that time for people to build economic models. The first factor was the comparative scarcity of economic statistics and the comparatively unorganized form of what statistics there were. I am not saying for a moment that there were no economic statistics, that there were no economic statisticians, and that a great deal was not achieved in the nineteenth century. But looked at by modern standards and by the requirements of almost any kind of economic model building, the going would have been very rough, and anyone who doubts this statement can try his hand at collecting the sort of information he needs for his model back of the first world war, or for that matter back of the second world war.

Another factor is that the techniques of statistical estimation were far less developed than they have since become, so that even if one had a good deal of data, one would have found it necessary to invent new methods for analyzing them. This is an effort which we economists have been to some extent spared, as many of the methods we need have in the meantime been developed by others.

Finally there is the factor of computing techniques, which I don't think should be — I don't suppose is likely to be — underestimated in this connection. The pre-war models, which in any case were not very numerous, were comparatively simple things, and solutions could be reached by means of desk calculators. With many of the models built nowadays this procedure is impossible because of the time it would take even a large computing staff to reach a solution. In the case of my own model in Cambridge, which deals with the British economy on a fairly detailed but still fairly aggregated basis, the calculations for a set of commodity balances of the kind that appear in *Exploring 1970* take a minute and a half computing time, on an electronic computer, but the number of sums that are done in that minute and a half would probably require sixty man-years with a desk calculator and therefore, obviously, would never be done.

These, I think, are some of the reasons why the world has been a bit slow to follow up the systematizing work of nearly a century ago. But if it has been slow to follow it up, it has certainly been almost unanimous in doing so once the idea had caught on. About three years ago I carried out an international survey of the economic models which were currently being built all over the world. I was not in a position to make a very complete survey: all I had to rely on were personal contacts and some knowledge of what people were doing. In answer to my questionnaire about the structure and character of the models, I received reports on about forty of them. No doubt there are many more. But those for which I did get replies were sufficiently widespread to confirm that this sort of activity is going on in most parts of the world, and in Europe and the USA on a fairly considerable scale. For anybody interested in the subject, a brief report of my survey was published recently in *National Economic Planning* by the National Bureau of Economic Research in New York.

And now I should like to offer a few general comments on some of the major issues of model building. To some extent I shall inevitably go over the ground which has already been covered by others, but perhaps here and there I shall be able to introduce something new. After that I should like to turn my attention to some of the technical problems which arise in model building, in order to illustrate a number of points which seem to me important. And finally I should like to say a few words about what we have been doing in Cambridge since we published *Exploring 1970* two years ago.

2 General issues

As regards the general comments, the first question I want to discuss is that of the scale on which model building activity should be carried out. Of course it is possible for one or two individuals to build a prototype model, and indeed the pre-war models and many models which have been built since have in fact been built in that way. But if one is going to set up a model in any degree of detail, the number of aspects that must be taken into account and the amount of data-processing which is involved make it absolutely essential to have a critical mass of resources on the job if any useful results are to come out. In other words I don't think it is any good, certainly in the field of general model building, to think in terms of very small units. In my survey the size of the units varied, but was generally in the range of six to twelve people. In many cases I think this figure was misleading because it related only to the central model building team and left out a number of people, perhaps in other government departments — many of these models are government models — who in fact were doing a large amount of data-processing for the central team. The man and a boy days are definitely over.

Perhaps even more important than the size of the group which is working on a model is the question of its continuity. As Professor Ball was saying this morning, in the early days people would build a model and then go and do something else. By contrast, the models which entered in my survey tended to be more or less continuing activities. The great advantage of this is that it gives the model builder an opportunity of learning from his model and improving it.

The third question is the point of departure. Unlike the other two, this does not seem to me to matter very much. Presumably one will start either from one's own interests or from the interests of the policy-group which has brought one into being. But the subject is so enormous that wherever one starts from, one will not be able to get very far in the first round of the exercise. One should, however, be able to find out some of the things which it is important to know about, and to put in the right perspective some of the things which people often talk about a great deal but which are not in fact really important. Models are useful both for understanding the system being modelled and for making predictions for policy and planning purposes. Exactly which of these is one's primary interest will no doubt affect where one begins. But it will be very difficult to stop anywhere along the line, and in time I imagine that the differences which seem so clear-cut nowadays between models set up in different centres and for apparently different purposes will be much less obvious in the future.

The fourth general question I want to talk about is the scope of models. Naturally most economic models are built by economists, and so the variables, the set-up, the way of looking at things are essentially economic. But economists are coming to realize more and more not merely that social and other non-economic factors are important — I think they have always realized that — but that they themselves should do something about them, should widen the scope of their models, not simply be content with the kind of relationships which traditionally appear in economic theory. The reason for this is not very hard to see : if one is applying a model to a real-world situation, one will not throw much light on it if one tries to analyze it in terms of a single discipline, paying no attention to other disciplines that are relevant. Indeed, in many cases, it seems to me, social factors and social institutions may be more important in determining the outcome of an economic situation than many of the things that economists feel more at home with.

My fifth question concerns organization. I don't know what the general opinion would be, but I have always supposed that the model that we are building in Cambridge is by most standards a fairly large one. Actually it is not very large, and in terms of the amount of detail necessary for accounting purposes in specific areas it is in fact rather small. Nevertheless, the amount of data-processing involved, even for a model with as few as thirty industries, forty consumption goods, twelve government purposes and five financial sectors, is quite terrific. And it is unthinkable, to my mind at least, that at the present stage one could contemplete setting up a really elaborate model and then proceed to get the information, define the relationships, estimate the parameters and reach a solution. In my opinion, if one wants more detail the right way to go about it is to pursue a policy of divide and conquer, that is to set up a system of submodels, each relating to a specific part of the economy that requires in itself a large amount of information. I do not believe that anyone could undertake the data-processing needed to produce a monolithic model, so to speak, in real detail.

My sixth and last general question has to do with co-operation. One thinks of the group of people who write the book or books in which the model is described as the model-building team. But in fact they are only part of the whole collection of people who in one way or another contribute to building the model. It is not possible for a team of six to twelve people, however well endowed, however industrious, to deal with all the problems that arise in the construction of a model. Above all, it is not possible for them to obtain unaided all the information they want or to form sensible views about every change in consumer habits, say, or every change in the technology of production. They are bound to need the assistance of people engaged in similar but more specialized work in specific branches of industry and government. I say these things because it seems to be extremely important to broaden the conception of model building, reach a better understanding of what it really involves and alter the climate of opinion and the social processes on which its success depends. I think the world has cottoned on to these ideas and is largely in agreement with them, but I also think that perhaps they are still worth a mention.

3 Technical problems

As regards the technical problems of model building, I should like to divide the field into four main categories. They are all very familiar: the specification of variables, the formulation of relationships, the estimation of parameters, and the calculation of a solution.

What can we say about the specification of variables? Well, it seems to me that in economic model building a matter of the first importance is to have a coherent framework for the variables which enter one's model. Furthermore, if one's intention is to build a variety of specialized models — one designed, let us say, for the examination of long-term prospects, another for the formulation of medium-term policy, a third for the control of short-term instability — it seems to me that the variables in these different models should be explicitly related to each other so as to link the models together. In an economic system there are a great many accounting and arithmetical identities which hold; and these should be clearly recognized as part of the foundations of the model building process.

From this point of view the development of social accounting has a great deal to offer. Indeed it is one of the prerequisites for the improvement of economic models. This is a matter which no individual can handle alone, particularly on a world-wide scale, which is how it should be handled because a great deal can be learnt about economic relationships from properly conceived international comparisons. For example, Dr. Kendall this morning spoke about the difficulty of getting satisfactory units, and quite right he is. I think the only way to achieve good results in this field is to evolve a highly systematic way of setting up information and to have as much discussion as possible among various people who in their different countries are trying to handle what are after all exactly the same problems. It is fortunate that various international agencies, particularly the United Nations, have taken up the task of constructing and keeping up to date a framework for economic variables, which can be consolidated or deconsolidated at will to make a smaller or larger number of aggregates in such a way that the relationships between the variables are clear. In the most recent work of the United Nations in this field, which I hope will be published before long, the comparatively simple *System of National Accounts* devised some fifteen years ago is being very much extended. It now integrates within a single framework information on stocks and balance sheets — which seems to have been singularly overlooked by economic statisticians in recent times — with information on flows. An accounting system of this kind is to a very large extent all-embracing in the sense that, while the flows and stocks in the accounts are expressed as sums of money, associated with those sums of money there are quantities, prices, rates of interest and so on.

Let us now turn to the formulation of relationships. Here by relationships I do not mean the accounting and arithmetical identities which I have just been talking about and which hold true by definition, but those relationships which are based on hypotheses and must be tested against observations. Although in economics there is a wide range of behavioural and technical relationships that have to be considered, I shall content myself with a single example, namely the relationships connecting saving with the factors that determine it. This example illustrates two of the more challenging problems that face the model builder: what to do when one has no direct measurement of an important variable, although in principle one knows how to measure it; and how to use non-observable variables — a subject which Dr. Kendall raised this morning.

In the past it has been usual to try to explain variations in saving in terms of income and income-like variables, without introducing wealth explicitly into the picture. The reason why wealth is ignored is not so much that it is considered unimportant as that in most countries there are no regular measurements of it. However, one can approximate real wealth by accumulating real saving. The resulting measure is little more than a trend yet the hypothesis that saving — the rate of change of wealth — depends on income and wealth leads to different and much more interesting conclusions than does the hypthesis that saving depends on income and time.

The second problem is illustrated by the distinction, originally drawn by Friedman, between the permanent component of income — and wealth — and the corresponding transient component. These two components are non-observable in the sense that they are certainly not measured and perhaps not measurable, but they can be worked into the preliminary formulation and can then be removed by suitable transformations and substitutions so that in the final formulation the parameters can be interpreted in terms of the influence of permanent and transient components. By doing this one may lose generality, but it is better than ignoring two undoubtedly significant variables.

When all these refinements have been introduced, it can indeed be shown that saving is a transform of lagged income. But it would be impossible to interpret this form of the relationship without a knowledge of how it had been constructed out of a number of explicit considerations. Anyone interested in following up this example will find an application to postwar saving in Britain in the last issue for 1966 of the Italian journal *L'industria*.

Passing now to the estimation of parameters, I shall again content myself with one example: the estimation of input-output coefficients.

What is normally done is, first, to draw up, through the processing of statistical information, a statement of the use of commodities in different industries in a particular year, and thus to find out how much of each commodity was needed in that year by each industry to produce one unit of output. This is mainly applied economic statistics; higher mathematical methods do not contribute much to solving the difficulties and problems of making a table of this kind.

The next step is to allow for changes in the coefficients. As with so many aspects of economic model building, when the technique of input-output was first developed people were extremely pleased to have an input-output table at all and just went ahead and used it without modification as a tool for projection. Of course the results often turned out to be disappointing because, although some coefficients do not change or change very slowly, some do change and change very quickly. So what is one to do?

Well, the first thing is just to look at the table one has made for the base year and notice which coefficients are big and which are small, and which seem to be specific to particular industries and which are spread out across the board; and then go as far as one can with other information in trying to bring the table up to date. One will never really get home on this, but there is quite a lot one can do.

The next thing is to go round to the expert in industry and get him either to comment on what one has done or simply to replace it by something better; and, still more important, discuss with him what technical changes are in the air and what effect they are likely to have on the coefficients he knows about. Provided one does not want to look too far ahead — not more than five years or so, let us say — one usually finds that people have definite expectations about technical changes and are quite happy to put their knowledge at the disposal of the model builder.

By a combination of these methods — the statistical and the conversational — one can get a certain distance. But in some cases one can get even further: even if one cannot set up a time-series for the whole table, one can set up partial time-series for some of the elements in the table and derive projections from these partial time-series by econometric methods. We have in fact done this for the fuel and power industries using data that cover a period of about fifteen years. In this study we have something like eight fuel products and twenty-five to thirty using sectors, which adds up to a very large number of coefficients. In order to see how far the changes which had taken place in the more important of these coefficients could be explained by econometric methods, we have concentrated on the substitution of oil for coal.

The assumptions on which this work is based can be said very simply. People who use these two fuels in large quantities are sensitive to their relative prices. At the same time they are already endowed with certain equipment which makes use of either one or the other fuel. Consequently, if a price change occurs which would make it more economical to substitute oil for coal, some users will do it quickly but some will not get round to it for a considerable time. Thus the process of substitution, and therefore the change in the input coefficients, will go fast at first and then gradually slow down as more and more users reach equilibrium; and if relative prices are frozen by a policy measure, say, it will slow down more rapidly and eventually come to a stop. In other words, one can represent the change in the use of these fuels by a stock-adjustment model in which the factor determining the equilibrium use of the two fuels is their price-ratio. To my mind this gives a much better idea of how the input coefficients might move in the future than would a simple extrapolation of trends, because it provides a plausible explanation of why they have moved in the past. This would certainly seem to be true in the particular case we have studied: for a period in the fifties the relative prices of oil and coal were moving in favour of oil, and users were changing their fuel mix at a certain rate; but for some time now the price ratio has been approximately stabilized and the rate of change has slowed down noticeably.

When all these steps have been taken to project the base-year table into the future, there will remain a number of loose ends which will have to be tied up before a balanced table is obtained. For this purpose we have evolved a mathematical procedure which makes it possible to adjust the entries so that they add up to the totals of intermediate inputs and outputs required to reach a certain level of total output. This method consists of finding for each row and each column of the table a multiplier which ensures that the constraints just mentioned are met; when working out the multipliers, all the coefficients deemed to be known more or less accurately are omitted, and are added back afterwards to complete the table.

The moral of this example is that in estimating parameters neither the highbrow nor the commonsense approach is sufficient in itself. Every kind of method, mathematical and non-mathematical, should be brought in if the best use is to be made of the limited knowledge available.

On the question of calculation I have only one thing to say. It is very desirable, of course, that the computing side should be well to the fore, that it should be recognized as an integral part of model building. But not so much in order to calculate a single solution as to explore several alternative solutions; in other words, to carry out sensitivity analyses of those things that seem important, so as to find out in advance how the economy would react if some of the assumptions which have been made were changed. To the man who says 'I don't see why I shouldn't do so and so, let the economy be the guinea pig', the model builder should answer 'No, let us work out what you want and see what would happen, let the model be the guinea pig'. This, and not the blueprint approach, seems to me the right way of using computable models for policy purposes.

4 The progress of the Cambridge growth model

This brings me to what we have been doing recently with the Cambridge growth model. When we published *Exploring 1970* two years ago, we demonstrated that one could put the whole thing together and get some results, but we were under no very great illusion as to the tentative character of our estimates. How far have we progressed since then?

Well, one of the things we have done has been to improve the accounting framework of the model by revising our original figures for 1960 and constructing two more social accounting matrices, one for 1954 and one for 1963. This has been mainly a matter of data-processing, a task on which I suppose we spend more time than on any other single aspect of the work. Which is not at all as it should be but, given the statistics one has, is inevitable.

In the course of reworking the material for 1960 and adding the other years we have taken the opportunity of doing two things. One is to extend the number of activities and commodities in the model. The other, which in the long run will perhaps prove more important, is to modify S A M on the lines proposed for the revision of the U.N. *System of National Accounts*. Although this work means even more data-processing, it is already apparent that in all kinds of ways it is well worth-while. One feature of it is that the financial side of the economy, which in the old S A M was accorded a very perfunctory treatment, is considerably expanded. This has been made possible by the great improvement in British financial statistics since the publication of the Radcliffe report.

But for many purposes the social accounting matrices we have evolved are still much too aggregated and compressed. To correct this defect we are making separate studies of specific industries. I have already mentioned our work on fuel and power. In the field of metals and engineering too we have taken our old model apart so as to look at these industries in greater detail; engineering, for instance, has been divided into twenty branches. But we have not yet integrated our detailed tables into the new S A M, and I don't know that we ever shall. The reason why I say this is that if we were to try to use this material for model building rather than as background information which enables us to break down certain sectors, it would be better to use it as a basis for a submodel. The development of a model-system, with a number of satellite models connected to each other by a central model, is a side of our work to which we intend to devote much more attention from now on. The way I see it, the interplay between submodels and central model in such a system would be roughly as follows.

E

Suppose one starts a general model off and grinds out a lot of activity levels for the different industry groups. One or more of these groups will be producing fuel and power, let us say, and will require fuel and power to do so. How much of each kind would depend on the mixture of technologies employed; for example, on the extent to which electricity is derived from coal or oil burning equipment or from water power or nuclear energy. If we know how much electricity is required in the economy as a whole, we can use a submodel to work out how it should be produced and hence what the cost structure of the electricity industry would be. This can be done either by reference to the constraints set by existing fuel and power policies or, better still, by minimizing the cost of producing electricity subject to the usual programming constraints. By the same method a revised cost structure can be worked out for each of the other fuel and power industries and substituted for the original cost structure in the general model. Any change will of course produce different activity levels in all the industries in the general model, and therefore different levels of total demand for the various kinds of fuel and power. The submodel will then be set in motion again to calculate the mixture of technologies best suited to meeting these revised demands. And so on until the information passing between the general model and the submodel ceases to change.

In principle, a submodel could be built for any industry group or other complex activity — such as the educational system or the health service — each submodel being linked to the others through the general model. Thus one could hope for the day when most of the work in a model-system would be done by submodels operated by people who really knew about the activities they were modelling, and when the general model would become simply an adjusting mechanism for keeping the submodels in step. I like this idea as an aim for model building much better than the more usual one of just expanding and elaborating the general model *ad infinitum*, for the simple reason that there is a limit beyond which no single model can be elaborated without becoming unmanageable.

Another field in which we have made some progress is that of price sensitivity. On the input-output side there had always been some price sensitivity implicit in changing coefficients, but until recently we had introduced it explicitly only in our consumer-demand relationships. Now we are beginning to introduce it explicitly also in our foreign trade relationships. In *Exploring 1970* we had a rather mechanistic way of fixing up foreign trade, if I can put it like that. Exports, that is foreign demands for British commodities, were not based on any demand analysis undertaken by us but rested largely on official projections, and were simply fed into the model as an exogenous variable. Imports were divided into two categories: complementary imports, that is commodities that cannot be produced in Britain, and competitive imports, that is commodities that could be produced in Britain. Complementary imports, excepting the small proportion that flows directly into final demand, were treated as indispensable intermediate inputs and related to production levels by input-output coefficients. Competitive imports were made to depend in the aggregate on the amount of foreign exchange left over after the cost of complementary imports and other outgoings had been met and a fixed surplus on current account allowed for; subject to this constraint, each commodity group was then squeezed or expanded differentially according to its past sensitiveness to balance-of-payments fluctuations.

What we are now doing is to replace this oversimplified treatment with proper demand relationships. We have made a start with imports, relating them to such variables as the total demand for each commodity group and, in the case of competitive commodities, the ratio of the foreign price to the British price. Sometimes we have found it necessary to set up little models of imports, production and stockbuilding and to allow for lags in prices. Two general conclusions emerge from all this. First, it appears that there is a considerable degree of price sensitivity in British import demand. Second, it appears that an increase in the ratio of imports to total demand can be brought about not only by a relative rise in British prices but also by an increase in British total demand. This second conclusion needs further examination : if it is only a cyclical phenomenon it is not very disturbing; but if it turns out to have a long-term significance it is more serious since it implies that, with rising total demand, the import ratio for competitive commodities will tend to rise. Unless similar forces are at work in the countries to which we export, such a tendency can only contribute to a worsening outlook for the balance of payments.

We have not yet got round to a similar study of export demand, but we are planning to do it soon and to base it on a classification of exports by commodity and destination. In the meantime we have made use of what is known about British export elasticities to make this aspect of foreign trade price-sensitive too. Consequently, in our latest projections, which go to 1972, we no longer need to impose a fixed surplus on current account initially, but can adjust home prices in relation to foreign prices so as to achieve a satisfactory balance of payments subject to given requirements for final demand.

5   Demographic accounting

And now my time is nearly up and I realize that, although I entitled my talk 'Economic and Social Modelling', I have not mentioned the social side at all. So I shall conclude by outlining what I have been doing on this subject at the Research Centre of King's College, Cambridge.

When one thinks of the amount of work that has been done in the last generation on accounting for economic flows and stocks, it is somewhat surprising that a similar effort has not been directed to accounting for flows and stocks of human beings, who are after all the *raison d'être* of any effort to improve economic performance. In an attempt to fill this gap, I have developed a demographic accounting system in which human flows are viewed as a dynamic input-output process : the flows into this year are composed partly of the survivors from last year and partly of the births and immigrations of this year; and the flows out of this year are composed partly of the deaths and emigrations of this year and partly of the survivors into next year. We can thus set up a system of linked matrices covering a series of years, in which the number of people that flow into each year is equal to the number of people that flow out of it. If we then divide the population by age and activity, we can trace the flows into and out of different activities at different ages.

So far, my colleagues and I have been working on ten matrices, five for boys and five for girls, relating to the school population of England and Wales in the years 1961 to 1965. We have twenty age-groups, from age nought to age nineteen, and six main activities, namely 'not at school' and five types of school : nursery and primary, secondary modern, grammar, comprehensive, and others. After the age of fourteen we have subdivided each type of school so as to distinguish between sixth formers and non-sixth formers and between school leavers who go on to further education and school leavers who don't.

Our approach has been to fill up these tables as best we could from the information available, so as to have a basis for discussion with experts on different aspects of the educational system. This approach is reminiscent of what I said above about the estimation of input-output coefficients. There is also another point of contact with input-output analysis : from a series of population accounting matrices it is possible to calculate transition proportions for the future, that is to say the proportions in which the people of a given age in a given activity will redistribute themselves among the various activities as they pass from one age-group to the next. Such information provides the basis for a Markov-chain type of projection model. Anyone interested in following up these ideas will find them discussed at greater length in the journal *Minerva*, No. III, Part 2, 1965, and No. IV, Part 3, 1966. A further article giving a numerical example — boys up to age nineteen in England and Wales in 1963-64 — will shortly appear in the same journal.

My specific aim in developing this system is to collate educational statistics in a way which will be useful for educational planning. My general aim is to bring together demographic, educational, manpower and other social statistics within a coherent framework, and eventually to link them with the economic model. But that is something for the future.

AN INTEGRATED MODEL OF AN OIL COMPANY

W. J. NEWBY

Interest in the use of mathematics for oil industry problems dates back to the application of linear programming to the blending of aviation gasolines in 1952. Since then, in step with the advance of computers and improved techniques, the subject has grown very rapidly within the industry. At present model building is a wide-spread activity covering practically all aspects of operations. The nature of the work and the approach vary considerably from one Company to another, ranging from the study of purely local matters for planning current and future operations to the solution of Company-wide problems.

The purpose of this talk is to outline briefly the approach adopted by British Petroleum and to describe some of the results.

The system

The facilities of the BP Company are numerous and world wide. They comprise a vast network of sources of crude oil, refineries, crude oil and product storage facilities and marketing outlets, linked by a complicated transport system of tankers, barges, pipelines and road haulage. The hub of the system is the refinery which converts crude oil into a variety of products such as chemical feedstocks, motor gasolines, heater oils, fuel oils, lubricants, bitumen, etc. The proportions and the qualities of the products made by the refineries depend on the nature of the crude oil (which varies considerably according to origin) and the processing steps adopted in the refinery. The pattern of products required varies extensively from one country to another and is subject to large seasonal fluctuations. A considerable flexibility is thus required in the manufacture of products and this is achieved by adjusting the pattern of crudes supplied to the refineries as well as the operation of the process plants.

Because of the scale and complexity of these operations, it is not possible to show a real system in any detail, but for the purposes of illustration the essential features of an Integrated Oil Company operation can be shown in a simplified manner as follows :-

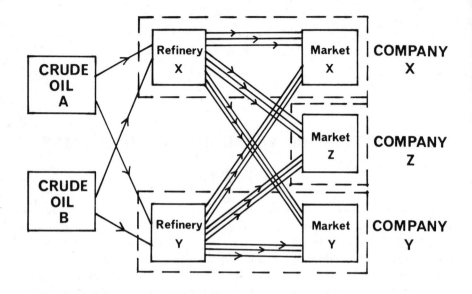

Fig. 1

Representation of a small integrated oil company

The diagram shows the logistics of the system. The Integrated Company illustrated owns two sources of crude oil, two associated companies engaged in refining and marketing, and a marketing company. For operational purposes, crude oils A & B can be supplied to either refinery in any appropriate proportion. Each refinery can manufacture products either for its local market X and Y or for the associate Company Z. Markets X and Y can take products either from its own refinery or from the other refinery. Market Z can take products from either refinery. For simplicity, the possibilities of purchase and exchange of crude and products from sources outside the group, and the sale of crude oil, etc, have been omitted.

For the next operating period, i.e. for an appropriate time period ahead, the decision and planning processes involve deciding on the supply of crude oils to the two refineries, the pattern of products to be made at each of the refineries, and from which refinery each market will be supplied. For moderate periods ahead the resources available to the companies will be known, and the demand for products firmly established, or capable of being predicted with reasonable accuracy. It will be evident that the various operations cannot be optimized without reference to the overall system.

The three associate companies X, Y and Z cannot optimize the Group operation by considering their own operations separately. Each will require knowledge of the others' activities for the same period. For example, any assumption by Company X about the level of production by Company Y pre-supposes that the best level of operation has already been determined for Company Y, and so on. The optimum levels of activity for the three companies, consistent with the resources available and the marketing requirements and opportunities, can only be established if all the relevant supply, refining and distribution alternatives are examined together. The planning procedure must therefore be comprehensive and a model designed for this purpose must, as far as possible, be constructed to solve an operationally complete problem.

The system is a physical one and one in which the relationships between the variables are known. By suitable formulation, all the relationships can be expressed in a linear form. For the purposes of optimization, in the short term operating period, the problem is to meet the total marketing requirement with the facilities and crudes available in the most profitable way. This can be achieved by minimizing the total cost of the overall operation, which is the familiar problem in linear programming of minimizing cost for a given volume of output. For the purposes of computation ease, only those costs which are relevant to the problem need be optimized and these are the cost of crude, freight, refinery chemicals, and transport to and within the markets.

Formulated in this way, the solution of the model will establish a practical programme for the operation of the total system for the appropriate operating period. This will consist of a set of interlocked programmes for each centre, including the quantity and origin of crude oils to be used by the two refineries, the sources of products for the three markets and, depending on the detail of the model, the refinery programmes and the distribution programme of products within the markets.

In model building the most complicated section of the model is the description of the refinery technology. For a single refinery, 100 - 200 linear equations are generally necessary to deal with the processing and blending relationships and for meeting the quantity and quality requirements of the products. A complete model for planning the short-term operations of the small company shown in the diagram would require about 400 equations containing 700 variables.

Very large linear models have been developed along these lines and are now being used as a matter of routine for planning the operations of most of B P's activities. Before describing these models it is necessary to discuss briefly the time scale of the planning period.

Time scale

The time span covered by the planning period is a prime consideration.

For short-term planning, e.g. 1 month ahead, facilities are known, trade is committed, and thus uncertainties over prices are not relevant. Because there is not time to build new facilities, the expenditure of capital is not a consideration. Short-term planning is therefore concerned with minimizing cost for a fixed demand. The dominant concern is the planning of operations to meet current trade. The problems to be solved for the long term are entirely different. None of the short-term circumstances is valid. The dominant consideration is what capital investments to make and when, such that these, when added to existing resources, will maximize future profits. The objectives and the circumstances are thus quite different according to the period of time in the future being examined.

For practical purposes it is convenient to consider the future in three time spans :-

Short term :	1, 2 & 3 months ahead
Medium term :	3, 6 - 12 months ahead
Long term :	2, 3 etc. years ahead.

For the shorter-term purposes, planning is concerned with making the best use of existing resources for reasonably close events. The nearer ahead one plans the more certain many factors become. On the other hand, particularly for a large system involving the movement of crude oil and products on a global scale, the operating period considered in the planning stage must be sufficiently distant to enable decisions to be implemented. For practical purposes this is 1, 2 & 3 months ahead for the variety of decisions involved in planning current operations, and 3, 6 & 12 months ahead for studying the opportunities for medium-term operations. Similar models are used for both these purposes, which are referred to as short- and medium-term estimating models. A separate model is used for long-term purposes. This is referred to as a long-term planning model, the essential difference being the ability to deal with capital, and the addition of new facilities.

To complete the picture there is the problem of day-to-day planning. In practice, even with close events, unexpected happenings and deviations from forecasts occur. Ships will not arrive on schedule or will break down; process plants will fail; the weather will change suddenly and alter the demand for products and so on. To a large extent, many of these unforeseen disturbances can be taken care of by tankage, and balances adjusted in the next planning period. But occasionally sizeable day-to-day variations in the planned operation, for one reason and another, are inevitable. Re-optimization of the whole system on the scale of operations involved and at short notice is obviously not a practicable proposition. Accommodation of the disturbance is therefore treated as a matter to be dealt with locally within the framework of the overall optimization for the

appropriate planning period. On-the-spot models of the local operations
are frequently used for these purposes, but these are separate from the
integrated types of model which are the subject of this talk, and represent
a second order of optimization.

Short - and medium-term models

Three main comprehensive models are currently in use in British
Petroleum for planning short- and medium-term operations.

(1) *Balancing Refineries System.* A global model of the deep-water
refineries and associated supply and marketing areas, dealing approximately with one million barrels/day refining capacity.

(2) *European Refineries System.* A European model of refining and
marketing in the main countries of the Continent of Europe dealing
approximately with 600 000 barrels/day of refining capacity and
giving particular emphasis to the overland distribution of products.

(3) *French Refineries System.* A model of the operations in France
which duplicates some of the operations in the European system, but
in considerably more detail.

Because of size these models cannot currently be computed as one
model, but there is a link between them through the marginal values
generated by the models for crudes and products. A comparison of these
values provides a basis for determining import/export balances between
the systems, for individual products, and for adjusting crude oil avail-
abilities.

The area covered by two of the models is approximately as follows :-

	Balancing system	**European system**
Refineries	Aden	Rotterdam (Holland)
	Gothenburg (Sweden)	Hamburg (Germany)
	Grangemouth (UK)	Ruhr (Germany)
	Llandarcy (UK)	Vohburg (Austria)
	Kent (UK)	Dunkirk (France)
	Kwinana (Australia)	Lavera (France)
	Westernport (Australia)	Strasbourg (France)
Shared refineries and processing	Abadan (Iran)	Antwerp (Belgium)
	Kuwait	Aigle (Switzerland)
	Milazzo (Italy)	Venice (Italy)
		Genoa (Italy)
		Ravenna (Italy)
		Etc.

	Balancing system	European system
Markets	Aden	Belgium
	Australia	Holland
	Japan	Germany
	N.W. Europe	Switzerland
	U.K.	Italy
	West Africa	France
	Etc.	Etc.

The matrix details for the two models are approximately as follows :-

	Rows × columns	Rows × columns
Crude Oil supply	70 × 70	110 × 160
Refining technology	920 × 1410	790 × 1920
Products supply	60 × 800	220 × 800
Miscellaneous	50 × 20	80 × 220
Matrix size	1100 × 2300	1200 × 3100

Computation

The models were originally computed on IBM 7090/94 equipment using C-E-I-R codes. Since 1966 the Atlas computer has been employed using a new LP code developed specifically for the purpose.

All short- and medium-term estimating is now carried out by these models and the procedure is well established as the normal method of Head Office planning. Since 1960, when the first version of the 'Balancing System' was commissioned, many hundreds of calculations have been completed. Short-term estimates are carried out monthly, for 1, 2 & 3 months ahead, and medium-term estimates, quarterly.

The preparation of the data and the updating of the models are shared by the appropriate Supply and Refineries Departments as a normal operating function. Compiling and the actual computing is carried out by a Computer Department in close collaboration with the operating departments. The nature of the input and the form of the output are briefly as follows :-

Input	Output
Crude oil availability	Crude oil programme
Product requirements	Refinery programmes
Refinery shutdowns	Product movements
Stock availability	Product exchanges
Charter availability	Stock decisions
New economic data	Cost data
New quality data	
Purchase and exchange agreements	

The results are summarized in 'plain language' by a 'report writer' which is shared by the main operating departments and centres in the Company.

Benefits

The cost of computing and the staff effort involved for the regular use of models on this scale is appreciable, but the savings and the advantages have more than outweighed the expense. Apart from new information about the technical and economic behaviour of the company, an appreciable reduction in operating costs has been achieved. This has been due to a better use of crude oils and refinery plant, better control of stocks, and more flexible supply arrangements for meeting the contingencies of trade or weather. Apart from the more obvious operating advantages for meeting current commitments, the model solutions produce a large amount of economic data about the operations of the Company. This includes relative values of crude oils and products, relative changes in Group costs for changes in operating and sales patterns, all of which are significant for shaping the commercial activities of the Company, particularly for the medium and long term.

Because of the vast amount of detail involved and the intricate nature of oil matters it is not possible to give full-scale examples to illustrate the nature of the benefits derived from the use of optimizing models. However, the following example illustrates the kind of improvement the introduction of rigorous mathematical methods introduces.

The example is taken from a demonstration exercise carried out in 1960 to test the use of computer methods using a model of a single refinery against the conventional hand methods of calculation then in use. Six estimators from refineries and key centres in the organization were given the same problem and the results compared with a computer model solution.

The problem was to calculate the quantity of three crudes for a typical refinery, for producing a specified quantity of main products and a maximum quantity of heater oil. The main products consisted of some 17 separate products covering the normal range of motor gasolines, diesel oils, fuel oil etc. The results for the six estimators and the computer are summarized in the following table.

Basis   *'000 tons/quarter*

Refining capacity :	765
Crude A :	Unlimited
Crude B :	300 Med. max.
Crude C :	410 Med. max.
Main products :	567 (17 grades as specified)
Heater oil :	Max.

Results

'000 tons/Quarter

	Crude	Main products	Heater oil	Total
Estimator A	655	567	NIL	567
Estimator B	671	583	26	609
Estimator C	751	567	112	679
Estimator D	745	567	111	678
Estimator E	743	567	107	674
Estimator F	749	567	113	680
Computer	764	567	129	696

The computer result speaks for itself. Even for the best conventional estimate the computer shows an increase in production of heater oil of 64 000 tons per annum, amounting to nearly 2 per cent on crude. This result relates to a single refinery and the result was born out in practice subsequently. When the first calculation of the 'Balancing Refinery System' was completed in 1960 a hidden possibility for the production of an additional million tons of heater oil was disclosed. This example relates to the production of heater oil which at that time was a product in short supply, but the principle applies to all products.

Long-term planning models

The major effort in the past in British Petroleum has been directed towards establishing short- and medium-term procedures as having the greatest potential for immediately improving the performance of the Company.

Attention is now being turned to long-term planning, making full use of the model-building experience and computational techniques available. A number of models are in various stages of use and development for these purposes. These reflect two separate approaches. The first is a logical development of the existing models in which the objective is to determine refinery and supply requirements for estimated forecasts of the future. Naturally, any change in assumption about the future, for example, what the sulphur requirements of fuel oil will be or what crude oils will be available, will produce different refinery and supply requirements. Which course to adopt, where immediate decisions are involved, is a matter of judgement. For the second approach the emphasis is being placed on the best use of capital for expanding refinery, supply, and marketing facilities for a particular marketing situation using optimization techniques.

These two methods represent a very practical approach to the complex problems of long-term planning and they are now beginning to be used on an extensive scale for long-term decision making. It is not intended to discuss these models in any detail as experience of their use in practice is still being accumulated.

References

[1] A. Charnes, W.W. Cooper, and B. Mellor, 'Blending Aviation Gasolines', *Econometrica*, Vol. 20 (April 1952).

[2] W.J. Newby and R.J. Deam, 'Optimization and Operational Research', Third Congress of the European Federation of Chemical Engineering, London, June 1962.

[3] W.J. Newby, 'Planning Refinery Production', Conference on Computable Models, organized by the British Computer Society, October 1964.

[4] P.B. Coaker, 'The Use of a Computer in the Operation of a Multi-Refinery System', presented at the Computer Conference, Dallas, Texas, October 1964.

[5] D.F. Mitchell, 'Experience: The Computer Behind Oil Supply' in the *New Scientist*, 18th November 1965.

PROBLEMS OF BUILDING A MODEL OF A COMPANY

A. S. NOBLE

CONTENTS

1 Introduction

1.1 The title of this paper was suggested to me by Dr. M.G. Kendall as perhaps a rather different contribution to this conference. The 'model' is very much in vogue as a tool for analysing national economic problems and business situations, and the literature on the construction and application of these models in various spheres of activity is rapidly leaving the would-be reader far behind. However, as an encouragement to the stragglers and, I hope, in the spirit of Dr. Kendall's invitation to me, this paper is offered not as a record of achievement in model making but as a presentation of many of the problems, some still unsolved, which may beset the ambitious who are rash enough to attempt to represent in mathematical-economic terms the activities of a large and complex business organization. My general theme is that although much has already been achieved, modelling of the firm in all its ramifications is still in its infancy and it behoves all the experts to avoid proclaiming the true managerial revolution before many shots have been fired in anger; my discussion, therefore, is mainly about what has still to be done, not what has been done.

1.2 But before that, I must emphasize that I am speaking personally and in generalisations. Compared with the major oil companies such as British Petroleum Ltd., I.C.I. Ltd. was somewhat slow in applying conventional linear programming models to its more diverse operations. Now, however, there are many such models throughout the Company and great progress is being made with the use of the modelling approach (not only LP) in the major decision-making areas. Because I have agreed to speak on the problems and difficulties, this does not mean that any particular set of these exist in my Company as distinct from any other, nor indeed that some of them have not already been overcome. I would not like you to draw definite conclusions about the 'state of the art' in I.C.I. Ltd.

from what I am going to say. However, I shall be speaking in the context of the large industrial organisation since most of my experience lies there.

2   What is a model of the firm?

2.1   This is a question which the would-be model builder is often asked and he is bound to reply not with an answer but with a whole string of questions of his own. There are as many models of the firm as there are major activity areas, and the models will differ in size, complexity and detail according to their proposed use, to the availability of data and to the approach of the model builder. Thus at the very start we are faced with a three-fold problem which is enough to daunt even the stout-hearted.

2.2   The principal activity areas are:

> Production
> Distribution & Inventory
> Sales
> Purchasing & Supply
> Marketing
> Capital Investment
> Finance
> Research & Development
> Personnel

Of course, these are all inter-related and one basic model structure may embrace several of them with emphasis in different places according to the application; for instance, a linear programming model can cover the first four although a detailed treatment throughout can lead to difficulties with size, ease of comprehension and interpretation to which I shall return later.

2.3   Not only can the firm be divided into its functional areas but also its organization can separate it into fairly independent (although possibly physically inter-linked) spheres of authority and responsibility in which all the functions are represented. The question of the organization of a company and the impact of model-building on it is another I shall deal with at greater length, but the point I want to bring out here is that organizational divisions either by function or because of historical development or for any other reason do provide natural areas in which to start the construction of models. However, the immediate objectives for the use of such models are often rather different from those of a company as a whole, and difficulties are bound to arise where links between the various sections of a company are broken by the application of conventional, often arbitrary, accountancy rules.

2.4   It is here, therefore, that the model builder has to make up his mind about his approach. Is he going to build a whole series of micro-models which will eventually be linked together or is he to attempt a much coarser macro-model? In many ways, the micro level is easier to work at and there is a temptation to think that the pursuit of every detail will certainly result in a better model which more closely represents the real-life situation. I myself think that the answer is to work at both levels at once. Although the first trials may be conducted at the micro-level, quite early in the development of company model building an attempt should be made to work 'from the top down' as well as 'from the bottom up'. We must beware of getting bogged down in a morass of detail which prevents us from identifying the major factors which influence a company's performance. There is no merit in detail and complexity as such.

2.5 To build a coarse model which has relevance, however, is difficult. In any large organization with a certain amount of decentralization, information reaching the centre is unlikely to be adequate for the purpose. This is not surprising since, as with a national economy, information is collected for other purposes, often largely for preparing regular financial statements. In spite of this, the aim should be to build an experimental tool which can clearly demonstrate the value of the modelling technique and can begin to give some inkling of the proper direction for further investigation.

2.6 The last question in this section is what sort of model of the firm are we to attempt to build. Is it to be for operational, tactical or strategic planning? Is it to be static or dynamic, deterministic or stochastic? Is it to be some sort of optimization model or simply descriptive and exploratory? Again, there are no universal answers. We are limited by the availability of data and the power of present techniques. I would identify three distinct types of model which are being used in my own Company and elsewhere:

> Mathematical programming models
> Simulation models
> Input-output models

These are optimizing, exploratory and descriptive in that order. The first and third types have tended to be static and deterministic while simulation has offered the only real possibility of examining dynamic and stochastic effects. As to the time span of the models, mathematical programming has been used largely in the operational and tactical planning fields, with some rather cumbersome excursions into strategic planning; simulation has a wider scope, but the design of proper experiments with the model is difficult; input-output analysis I regard as a means of increasing our understanding of the structure of a company and its place in its industry and in the economy as a whole. For the last, I suggest we should be seeking means of making models of the economy compatible with models of at least the large companies.

F

2.7 In identifying the various types of models, I have left out of consideration decision models, that is, models of decision processes themselves. This is an important class of models and I look to a rapid growth in the use of decision tables and decision trees together with a further developed theory of games. However, I defend my omission by saying that such models are not models of a company.

2.8 To sum up, therefore, at this time we cannot think in terms of a single model of the firm. Within our present abilities, modelling has probably four strands which gradually become interwoven: for the physical resources of a company, an input-output model is a useful analytical tool as a preliminary to a mathematical programming (in the first instance, usually linear programming) model applicable to tactical planning; for strategic market and capital investment planning, an ad hoc approach which may be based on mathematical programming is probably the best we can do; for financial planning, simulation models are appropriate for studying the financial behaviour of the firm in relation to its shareholders, customers and suppliers, such models to be linked in some way with strategic planning models.

3   Construction and implementation

3.1 Although there is an enormous amount of research still to be done, there is much we can do now even with our limited technical resources. Models of the firm or of substantial parts of it are technically feasible, and by far the greatest problems lie in obtaining suitable data and in the creation of an organization which can effectively interpret and implement results.

3.2 Here, a word is in order about human resources for model building. In desperately short supply are people with suitable training and with a flair for problem analysis which is above simply great ability in any particular discipline. Not all of these are available for this activity and those that are require to add experience to their natural gifts. Experience is the most valuable asset and should not lightly be wasted. I suggest, therefore, that companies which are serious about model building have to keep their expert personnel in the one activity for a reasonably long, continuous period. If done properly this should not have a narrowing influence on the individual. While a strong team is laboriously being gathered together (and this is a slow process) I would commend to you the use of the best consultants in the field. I am happy, too, to pay a compliment to the organisers of this conference in recognition of the considerable contribution of their senior consultants to the development of modelling techniques.

3.3 What, then, are the problems of model construction? First, we require data on the structure of the company — plants in existence and planned and their characteristics, raw materials and intermediates used in manufacture, methods of transportation, customers' location and requirements. For a large firm this represents many hundreds of thousands of items of data, but apart from the sheer labour involved in collection, the data are not really difficult to obtain as a once-off exercise. What can be extraordinarily difficult is to ensure that the data are regularly kept up to date. It will often happen that a well designed data collection system is lacking because large scale modelling is still experimental and the experimental stage will last longer than necessary because there is no system. This, I fear, is a burden which the innovator must bear.

3.4 The other major requirement is for financial data, costs and revenues of various kinds. This is the first of two areas where the model-building activity impinges on the accounting function of a company. The accountant, because he is mainly concerned with reporting historical results, produces reports containing average costs (variable and fixed) and average selling prices (U.K. market, export markets). Again, 'full cost' is made of items arbitrarily allocated. The model builder, of course, wants data which will allow him to calculate the true relationship between output and costs, between sales and revenues. In some cases the former relationship is impossible to obtain except by lengthy and possibly expensive experimentation with production plant; but it is something that will become increasingly necessary as the use of models becomes more widespread.

3.5 It has become a common sport of Operational Research workers to belittle the accountancy profession in its approach to so-called management accounting. Let me make it clear that I am not one of those who participate in this sport. In my view, it is most important that the best accountants participate fully in model building. I believe that the much vaunted 'mixed-team' approach is really the best for this activity and it should provide one of the training grounds for company managers of the future.

3.6 This leads me to consider the problems of the successful application of models to a company's business. It involves on the part of managers comprehension of the objectives and of the methods, education in the use of models and in the interpretation of the results. But the responsibility is not on one side. The modelling expert must be able to communicate his ideas effectively. He must simplify wherever possible without seriously impairing the value of his models in tackling real problems and he must do everything he can to ease the task of interpretation. As the system being modelled becomes more complex, this can be a considerable task, but here I would reiterate Dr. Kendall's remark that the results obtained from a complex model are not necessarily themselves complex. Indeed, one should hope that the modelling of complex systems should make it possible to formulate a set of rules for managing the system which avoid the necessity of having continuous recourse to the model for assistance. Might it not be true that the best thing the model builder can do is to work himself out of a job? We should always remember, however, that just as important as any numerical results it may produce is the ability of a model to give us a real understanding and 'feel' for a complex business system.

3.7   I must return now to the problem of compatibility between the model builder and the accountant. The approach of the latter to a highly integrated production and distribution system is to break the links at places largely dictated by the organizational structure and to allocate costs both within and between the sub-systems in what appears to be a sensible, if arbitrary, way. Thus it is customary to speak in industry of the cost per ton of a certain intermediate or final product and of the profit per ton arising from some sale. This is a convenient way of summarizing the financial outcome of some set of operations in the past, but it can be quite useless for indicating to particular individual managers what they should do in the future. Here we enter the realm of the model, of 'opportunity cost' and of true management accounting. One of the great problems of accountancy seems to me to be how to devise an accounting system which will motivate managers to behave in the 'best' way for the whole organization (as indicated, say, by a company model) when they themselves have control of and responsibility for only a part. This problem surely can be solved by the collaboration of mathematicians, economists and accountants. It will certainly mean that companies will have to 'keep more than one set of books' and the slightly nasty suspicion which this phrase arouses should be most firmly suppressed.

3.8   Model building is often regarded as a technical rather than a commercial activity. This distinction between technical and commecial which is still reflected in today's computer jargon is a most unhelpful one. The essence of a company model is that it processes large amounts of data, and to talk of its computing requirements in the same breath as those of pure technical computing is to continue to fail to recognize, as I believe many model builders have done so far, that it is now an absolute necessity to think of large models as part of a comprehensive data-processing system. I do not mean by that the mirage-like 'total systems' which are always five years in the future, but simply a proper file-processing approach to the problem of data handling. One of the keys to the successful application of large models is speed of response when a question is posed. This will be achieved only if the data are on-hand (or perhaps I should say on magnetic file) and up-to-date so that they do not take three or four days to collect, and if the output of results is immediately comprehensible. You should note that I draw a distinction between the computer system to handle the data and the organization system to make it available.

3.9 But in one important way large systems are unlike the usual D.P. systems. They are not routine but make irregular demands for large slices of time from powerful computers. This is likely to cause difficulty particularly in the 'mixed computer shops' now in vogue, especially so because unlike the conventional D.P. application, model systems cannot be tested by means of short files of sample data. Every test requires every item of data and may take just as long as any production run. The day must be very near when many companies, if they wish to construct and use large models, will have to assign at least one fairly powerful computer solely for that purpose.

4   Objectives

4.1 I have dwelt too long, perhaps, on what might be termed the mechanistic problems of company model building. Let us now look further at the kinds of models which may be useful and some of the almost philosophical problems which have still to be solved.

4.2 When we embark on the task of building models of a company, one of the first things we have to get clear is the objective of the organization. Here are a few from which to choose :

> Maximize short-run profit
> Maximize long-run profit
> Maximize the return to shareholders
> Maximize growth subject to a 'satisfactory'
>   level of dividends

and there are many more not all of which contain the magic word 'maximize'. It certainly is a mistake to think that the objective, or perhaps more properly I should say objectives, of his company are clearly before every manager each time he takes a decision or prepares his plans. Nonetheless, for a model we clearly do need to have some criterion by which we can compare one possible result with another.

4.3 One approach is to have an objective function which we then proceed to maximize subject to various constraints. It is by no means certain, however, that maximization of anything is the aim of the company — more important may be a plan which is robust against the vagaries and vicissitudes of an uncertain world. Or again, it might be true to say that we are trying to maximize something but we are not sure what. In any case maximization implies a time-span and this is almost impossible to define. Do we, therefore, evade this difficulty in a way by the use of discount factors on the value of money or by the 'horizon-year' method? These, I feel, are in fact ducking the issue although, in the absence of anything better, I would favour the setting of long-term goals for a company which are a matter for high level policy decisions arrived at with or without the assistance of models. The real use of the model is then to determine within the known constraints the 'best' path to follow, although I still hesitate to define 'best'. This ought to be a continuous process with the optimization criterion possibly changing according to the company's situation.

4.4 I mentioned a moment ago the uncertain world. This is the real world which the model builder at the moment so often conveniently forgets because of the inadequacy of his tools. I am not saying that this is always wrong in that important results cannot be obtained by ignoring the uncertain nature of so many of the variables in the problem. However, we urgently require a breakthrough in methods of building and solving models which have stochastic elements and in which the variables are described by probability density functions. And not only the variables — the constraints may be in probabilistic terms and so may the objective function. Nor is this all, for the entire system may be constrained by strict equality relationships (e.g. material balances) which make the variables interdependent in complicated ways.

4.5 The econometricians have long been familiar with lagged variables and the dynamic representation of economic systems. The company model builder has the advantage in the matter of the availability of data, albeit difficulties remain, but he comes against precisely the same problems when he considers, as he must, the place of the company in the national economy or even in the world economy. So far, too little attention has been paid to the application of control theory to business systems, and I foresee the control engineer and the statistician having a large part to play in future developments.

4.6 One part of the outside world which is vital to the life of a company is its markets. Unfortunately, their behaviour and characteristics in the presence of competition have yielded hardly at all to mathematico-economic analysis. By now, you may have noticed my silence on this subject and this silence is because to my knowledge so little that is worthwhile has been done in the market modelling field. Short-term forecasting and the measurement of response to advertising are the exceptions that prove the rule. I need hardly say that this is a serious weakness which must prevent us from obtaining full value from company models for some time to come. I am hopeful, however, that econometrics will have a lot to offer here particularly in improving our insight into price-volume relationships.

4.7 Within the company, too, there is almost virgin territory for the model maker. This is the field of research and development, so important to a company like my own and to many others. The whole problem of the best allocation of resources to research projects, in competition with one another and with other uses for money, is one which still defies us although much has been written and said on the topic. I fear many more words will flow before we have success.

5   Organizational implications

5.1   I promised to examine the impact of company models on company organization and I venture to suggest that the effects could be quite far reaching in the long run. It is a trite remark to say that an organization consists of people, but nevertheless the model builder would do well to bear this fact very clearly in mind. His technology is only one of several which could affect organization, and there are important psychological and sociological factors as well.

5.2   People are best managed in fairly small groups, a model takes a global view; a manager reacts most favourably to responsibility *and* authority combined, a model may tend to remove that feeling of independence; human communication and human 'nous' must play an important part in business affairs, a model represents a scientific dehumanized system which cannot possibly reduce everything to mathematical relationships. At the end of last year 'The Times' newspaper reported that I.C.I. Ltd. would soon have models capable of conducting the affairs of the entire company. Let me hasten to assure you that this is not so, nor do I, a professional model builder, believe that this would be desirable even if it were feasible some time in the future. What in fact we require is a system in which model and human are closely integrated so that a free two-way flow of information can occur. No doubt routine decision will be taken over completely by machine, but the scale of business enterprises in the future will require *more* managerial and enterpreneurial skill, not less.

5.3   So the organization of a company will have to balance a number of conflicting factors. There may be a tendency to centralize certain activities such as strategic planning but operational control might become completely decentralized. In these circumstances the model builder is presented with a great challenge. Given that models exist for the company as a whole and for each of the operational units, how does one level link in with the rest? Ideally, we want to use a model at one level to set goals for the next level down, perhaps a whole hierarchy of models for company, division, works and plant. We want to set the goals but not the means of achieving them, or in other words we require a system of models which can be adapted for use in an organizational framework chosen for other reasons and which allows freedom of action to the individual manager within certain limits. Still the question remains – how can it be done? This problem, of course is closely related to the management accountancy one which I mentioned earlier.

6   Conclusion

6.1   In this paper I have ranged rather widely, dipping almost at random into several of the black boxes which litter the model building field. There are doubtless others from which you would like the lids lifted in discussion, but whether I can exorcize the demons which fly out remains to be seen.

6.2   I hope you do not feel that I have struck a pessimistic note. Quite the contrary was my intention. In this conference we are trying to be honest with ourselves about the true capabilities of models now and their likely future development. I myself am extremely optimistic about the outcome, but certain conditions will have to obtain before we can look back in ten years' time and wonder how on earth we had the problems we now face. The first of these is that a greater weight of mathematical and economic talent, together with expertise in other disciplines will have to study some of the fundamental problems. This could well imply even greater co-operation between industry and the universities. Second, Government and industry will soon have to start thinking much more positively about modelling and be organizing to do it and to use its results. Third, our very scarce resources for this activity may have to become, by some mechanism, more concentrated in the short term so that we can more quickly reach the 'take-off point'. Yet we must beware of introducing retrograde rigidity in the name of progress.

6.3   This seems to me to be one of today's most exciting fields of endeavour and success will bring great rewards to the whole community. I hope this conference is the first of many, each successive one of which will see an increase in our knowledge and the disappearance of more and more of the problems I have discussed this afternoon.

MODELS FOR TRAFFIC IN ROME

G. POMPILJ

Between July 1965 and November 1966 the Istituto di Calcolo delle Probabilità of Rome University elaborated two models for traffic in Rome [1]:

- one for the evaluation of the direct and indirect effects of possible restriction and control on traffic ; this I shall refer to as V I T (Valutazione Interventi Traffico) ;

- the other to predict the demand for traffic in the future ; I shall refer to this model as P O D S (Previsione Origine Destinazione Spostamenti).

These models utilize, among others, the results of the three inquiries which today, according to an experimental methodology already devised [2], are at the basis of every operative research on traffic :

(1) Origin Destination of trips (O.D.)
(2) Land Use (L.U.)
(3) Transportation Facilities (T.F.)

---

[1] The study was conducted by a Research Group formed, in alphabetical order, by: Dr. Roberto Beretta (Urban Architect), Mr. Massimiliano Bertucci (Statistician), Dr. Paolo Cutillo (Statistician), Dr. Francesco Gori (Analyst), Dr. Otello Iolita (Urban Architect), Dr. Franco Marta (Statistician), and has availed itself of the assistance of the following external experts: Dr. Giovanni Barillà, Com. te Prof. Walter Bisi, Dr. Aldo Cuzzer, Prof. Giorgio Dall'Aglio, Dr. Gastone Ferrara, Dr. Franco Fiorelli, Dr. Franco Giusti, Prof. Antonio Golini, Mr. Enrico Nervegna, Dr. Sergio Passeggieri, Dr. Ludovico Piccinato, Dr. Anna Portoghesi, Dr. Sergio Sturni.

[2] See e.g. *Chicago Area Transportation Studies*, Report in 3 Volumes, issued by the Government Authorities of the State of Illinois, 1959, 60, 62 ; *Pittsburgh Area Transportation Studies*, Report in 2 Volumes, issued by the Government Authorities of the State of Pennsylvania, 1962, 63; *Traffic in Towns*, Report by the 'Steering Group' and the 'Working Group' set up by the British Ministry of Transport, 1963 ; *London Traffic Survey*, Report issued by the London County Council and the British Ministry of Transport, Vol. 1, 1964; B.V. Martin, F.M. Menos, A.J. Bone, *Principles and Techniques of predicting Future demand for Urban Area Transportation*, M I T Press, Cambridge Mass ; IV Edition 1965. In this last volume is a bibliography, with a short summary, concerning 196 specialized works on the subject published in the U S A from 1948 to 1964.

These inquiries have been carried out mostly by the Municipal Statistics Department of Rome under the control of a special Committee under the chairmanship of B. BARBERI.

In this paper I shall give a brief account of the structure of the first of the two above mentioned models (VIT) confining myself to quote, in the last paragraph, the essential characteristics of the other model (PODS), which has been developed along the lines of experiences acquired elsewhere. [3]

1. Purpose of VIT. As already stated, VIT is a traffic model intended to evaluate the direct and indirect effects of possible restriction and control of traffic as, for instance, the creation of zones without vehicle traffic, of roads for one-way traffic, of routes controlled by traffic lights, of separate lanes for public transport vehicles, of building of subways, etc.

VIT is essentially based on a *graph* which represents synthetically the town street network and on a *program* [4] which, by using a powerful electronic computer, permits distribution on the graph of the requirements of traffic forecasted by the O.D. surveys. To each link of the graph some parameters are associated through the T.F. inquiry which, by characterizing the link, allow the above distribution to be made. The restrictions or controls on traffic alter such parameters in a way that, by simply replacing some values with others, it will be possible not only to reproduce the situation which we would have if a given intervention should take place but also, by redistributing the traffic on the basis of the new parameters, predetermine the repercussions, favourable or unfavourable, of the changed situation.

To illustrate what I have said up to this point, it is well to consider, before we go further, a fictitious example.

Let us presume that a project is suggested for the construction of a subway for vehicles. This intervention in the form of a new facility, once carried out, will cause as direct consequence a greater fluidity of traffic inside the zone of application; and many drivers, attracted by the possibility of saving time, will converge towards that zone, abandoning their former routes. There will follow a change in the distribution of traffic with repercussions which concern not only the zone where the subway is being built, but also far away zones.

---

[3] See e.g. the volumes, already mentioned in [2] about the traffic in the cities of Chicago and Pittsburg.

[4] The program, prepared in FORTRAN for ELEA 6001 by Dr. Gori, is reproduced in the Appendix.

If it were possible to know all this before the project gets to its operative stage, one could find the way to remove in advance, that is without waiting to see them, the possible negative effects of the intervention; one could even appreciate the convenience of building that subway. If, in the end, from this previous estimate it should be clear that the balance of advantages and disadvantages should not justify the cost of the work, the project could be dropped altogether.

Well, VIT, applied to the problem of that subway for vehicles, would allow us to measure in advance the effects of that construction. In fact, the greater fluidity of the traffic will be prepresented by suitable alterations of the values of the parameters concerning the links directly interested; in their turn, these values of parameters will change the distribution, on the graph, of the requirements of traffic forecasted by the O.D. inquiry; finally, the study of this new distribution will point out possible friction points, and possible negative repercussions.

2 Zoning. Research on town traffic requires that the whole territory of the town is divided into a certain number of zones (of suitable dimensions) and usually it is imagined that the phenomenon linked to those zones be concentrated at the centre of gravity of the same zone. For Rome, its territory is traditionally divided into 'quartieri' (districts) 'rioni' (boroughs), and 'suburbi' (suburbs); but these areas are all too wide with respect to our study. On the contrary, the net of 4,016 census areas has appeared far too detailed, though it is a very important basis for the L.U. inquiry.

Hence the Institute of Probability has divided the whole municipal territory into 733 zones with a view to satisfying the following principles:

(a) each zone is formed by grouping one or more neighbouring census areas, so as to facilitate the passage from results by areas to results by zones;

(b) each zone falls on only one district, borough or suburb, so as to reconstruct, when required, the data concerning these sections by simply adding those concerning the respective zones;

(c) when grouping the census areas, it has been tried to obtain such zones that would be most homogeneous from a standpoint of their functions, having in mind at the same time the present situation and the indications of the Town Development Plan, plus the number of arrivals in the 24 hours.

Of course it was not possible to avoid a certain amount of approximation as to the boundaries of the zones, which have been styles using a rather dense net; and as to the characterization of the functions, which has been occasionally impossible owing to the overlapping of functions in the same census area.

The net just mentioned supplies a monometric reference system with which the co-ordinates of the zone centre of gravity can be obtained. These co-ordinates, placing the origin so as to include in the first quadrant the municipal territory, have been expressed by positive integer numbers with a maximum of three figures. It has thus been possible to indicate each zone with a number of six figures of which the first three represent the abscissae and the others the ordinates of its centre of gravity.

The zones which are internal to the 'Grande Raccordo Anulare' (connecting road circling the town) are 643 and the remaining 90 are external. The 733 zones formed the basis for all the analysis the Institute has been doing; however they have been further grouped into 192 *study areas*, particularly useful for the representation of those phenomena which do not require a too deep analysis.

When determining the zoning on the basis of the above-stated criteria, we were quite conscious of the disadvantage of finding the main highways as boundaries between the zones; that is as a separating element. In the case of research on traffic it would have been better to have a zoning where the major streets had crossed the zone, thereby having a function of connecting elements.

On the other hand, by ignoring said criteria, no utilization could be made of either the data of the 1961 census or all other information already possessed by the municipal offices and this loss would have to be considered in relation to the more rational zonization.

3 The Graph. The traffic is made up of two components: one dynamic (represented by the flow of the trips) and one static (represented by the road net along which the trips are effected).

The necessary information on the trips is given by the O.D. enquiry whereas for the road net the results of the T.F. enquiry can be utilized.

VIT takes into account these components and provides thus a rational way for utilizing the results of the two inquiries at the moment when any decision is to be made as regards town traffic.

But it is at once evident that it is impossible to take into account the whole of the road net owing to the extreme complications involved. Hence the necessity to build a pattern which in some way meets both requirements, obviously contrasting, of handiness and of the respect for the real situation. From the contrast of these two requirements, a graph evolved which has as vertices the centres of gravity of the above 733 zones and as links the conjunctions of the centres of the adjoining zones, provided the road system and the traffic regulations permit passage from one to the other zone.

The links, numbering 2696, represent synthetically the whole network of the streets which connect, in the due direction, the two zones whose centres of gravity form the extremes of the same link. In this manner — by symbolizing with only one link a combination of streets (often a large number) — the road net of the town is much simplified, thus meeting that requirement of handiness just mentioned. In that picture the vertices of the graph do not stand for street junctions, nor do the links represent roads, but systems of roads.

The essential nature of the situation is satisfied by giving to each link of the graph three parameters, which in fact take into account the real situation shown in the actual link. These parameters are:

(1) length d (in metres), given by the mean distance on the road, between the principal centres of the two zones whose centre of gravity are at the end of the link;

(2) the number c of traffic lanes or tracks available on the road; this is a parameter, especially useful because it takes synthetically into account both the number of the roads represented in the link and their width;

(3) the initial speed v_0 (in metres per second), taken on a clear road, but taking into account information received on the specific road junction; such as frequency of crossings, the inclination of the roads, their paving, etc.

The number c of the traffic lanes will be not smaller than one because when it is, $c = 0$, the corresponding link in the graph will be missing.

In order to simplify the program to be inserted into the electronic computer, with which the allocation of the traffic is to be made, these three parameters have been in the first instance combined in order to form two new parameters which will then form the basis for the calculation of the final parameters. Of the two new parameters, one of them $t^{(0)}$ (in seconds), depends on the initial speed and upon the distance:

$$t^{(0)} = d/v_0$$

the other, $N^{(0)}$ (vehicles per hour), depends on the initial speed and on the number of the traffic lanes [5]:

---

[5] In order to understand the meaning of $N^{(0)}$ let us observe that:

— the coefficient $[1 + 0.8\,(c - 1)]$ is the number of the lanes, slightly reduced to take into account the fact that, all other conditions being equal, the 'capacity' of a road grows less rapidly than the number of the lanes;

— the numerator $3600\,v_0$ represents (in metres) the distance travelled in an hour by a vehicle moving at uniform speed v_0 (metres/second);

— the denominator $4 + v_0$ represents (in metres) the mean safety distance between
(continued on the next page)

$$N^{(0)} = \left[1 + 0 \cdot 8 \ (c - 1) \right] 3600 v_0 / (4 + v_0)$$

The parameter $t^{(0)}$ stands for the initial journey time, while the parameter $N^{(0)}$ states, for each direction of traffic, the theoretical maximum capacity.

All the above parameters are obtainable from the results of the T.F. inquiry. This inquiry also supplies information about public transport, which covers determined runs with determined frequencies; therefore it is known from the outset what the obstruction is, hour by hour, that they will cause on the different links. These data, which will be utilized when considering the flow of trips, are consequently part of another category of parameters of which we will speak later because they depend not only on the link of the graph but also on the interval of time to which they refer.

4 The times of covering the distance. The two parameters t_0 and $N^{(0)}$ enable us to express the time t required to cover the distance of a link as a function of the intensity N of the demand of traffic (number of passages per hour) to which the link is subject.

For these functions, the specialized literature suggests different expressions which may be grouped in the following three principal types:

$$t = t^{(0)} \ (1 + k_1 N) \qquad \text{(linear model)}$$

$$t = t^{(0)} \ (1 + k_2 N + k_3 N^2) \quad \text{(quadratic model)}$$

$$t = t^{(0)} e^{k4N} \qquad \text{(exponential model)}$$

Actually, the function which gives the time t of travelling the distance in the function of the intensity (N) of the demand of traffic should become infinite for $N > N^{(0)}$; but from a practical point of view it will suffice that t be large with respect to $t^{(0)}$. Moreover, a finite time (instead of infinite) affords a better reproduction of the real situation because, though taking more time, at the end they all pass; and because the presence of the obstruction, and therefore the forecast of a long time to travel the distance, induces the user of the road to change itinerary almost with the same force of persuasion as the conviction that the time has become infinite.

(continued from previous page)

the initial (or final) positions of two motor vehicles proceeding in the same direction at a speed v_0; this distance is formed by the mean length of the motor vehicle (m.4) and by the distance travelled in the 'reaction time', valued in one second (m.v_0).

The exponential model appears to be the one which best describes the variable data which is available; however, for the use intended of such relations in the operative scheme which we are examining here, the linear model appears to give an approximative more than sufficient, so much so as to insert it right away in the structure of the model.

As for the parameter k_1 it can be observed that, as in the general theory of the congestion, there are two principal causes producing increases in the times of travelling a distance as the demand for passages increases: irregular formation of the demand (which is not uniform in the considered interval of time) and indiscipline of the road users. The combined effect of these two causes is such that the traffic situation becomes considerably heavy when $N = 1/2 N^{(0)}$. For these reasons, the following function is suggested:

$$t = t^{(0)} \left[1 + (6/N^{(0)}) N \right] \qquad (1)$$

which for $N = 1/2 N^{(0)}$ gives $t = 4t^{(0)}$ and for $N = N^{(0)}$ gives $t = 7t^{(0)}$; this is a period of duration which is practically prohibitive.

Taking this into account, the following two parameters are attached to each link:

$$t^{(0)} = d/v_0$$

$$k = 6/N^{(0)}$$

which form a first category of information to be given to the computer in order to characterize the graph.

I will also recall, before passing to a further subject, that if some direction, for want of roads or for traffic regulations, is not possible ($c = 0$) we will not consider the corresponding link in the graph.

5 Assignment of trips.

The O.D. inquiry supplies, for a fixed interval of time, the number of trips between each pair of vertices on the graph, taken in order as origin and destination of the trip.

This inquiry does not give the route over which the trips have been effected since this information is not relevant as the routes are closely connected with the road situation at the moment when the trip took place.

The problem remains to allocate according to realistic criteria, a route for each trip. In this section I deal with this point with reference to the journeys of motor vehicles.

The allocation can be made in a great number of different ways and thus, first of all, the general criteria have to be determined upon which to build a given allocation rather than another.

It is first to be noted that within the limit of one hour's interval, when a precise route is attributed to each trip, the single links of the graph will be loaded with an (hourly) demand of traffic, equal, for each direction, to the number of the trips using them. Calling γ_{ij} the oriented link which connects the vertex i with the vertex j, it will be found that N_{ij} trips make use of the link $_{ij}$ and it will be possible to calculate by means of (1), the time to cover the distance, say t_{ij}, relating to that link. The total time, required by the aggregate of all the foreseen trips will be then given by

$$\Sigma_{ij} \, N_{ij} \, t_{ij} \tag{2}$$

and its value depends on the way in which a route has been allocated to each journey.

Among all possible allocations, the one appears preferable for which the total (2) is minimum. This manner of proceeding corresponds to the hypothesis that all road users will choose the most convenient route in respect of duration; this hypothesis is sufficiently realistic, even if not completely acceptable in the rigid definition I have given above. It is in fact legitimate to think that motorists, mostly for their most frequent journeys, will ultimately recognize the most convenient route, in time saving as compared with the traffic situation which they come up against, thereby possibly causing some excess of crowding on the route which would have been preferable in case of a smaller demand for traffic. Be it further remarked that the above rule of assignment does not lead in general to a single route, in order to go from one vertex A_i to a vertex A_j but leaves to the single user a certain freedom of choice among many routes and the only condition that the choices spread in such a way as to not cause excessive loads on certain links.

The consideration may be reckoned as valid only for private motor vehicles since the public vehicles have to follow determined routes with certain criteria quite different from the one just mentioned. However, in this case, the routes are known for sure (T.F. inquiry) and it may be reckoned, for each link of the graph, the number of passages of public transport vehicles in the interval of time being considered. Evidently the obstruction caused to the traffic by a public transport vehicle cannot be assimilated to that caused by an ordinary private vehicle, both for its dimensions and for the fact of being compelled to stop at fixed points; it is therefore necessary to render the two flows homogeneous, by multiplying the number of the public vehicles by proper coefficients. In the case of traffic in Rome for buses and trolley buses, the coefficient 4 has been used; whereas for trams the coefficient used was 6.

A separate account is finally required for 'goods transportation'; in fact not all links γ_{ij} are available, in a given hour, for the transportation of goods on certain types of lorries; and it is obvious that for the links where this is possible, the lorries contribute to make traffic worse. This traffic also requires being made homogeneous with that of the private motor vehicles by multiplying by proper coefficients the relevant demand for traffic between the couples A_r and A_s of vertices; moreover to attribute to these vehicles the same speed as that of the private vehicles is a mere convention not influencing the efficiency of our model.

Summing up we have a second series of data to give to the computer, strictly linked to the hour of the day to which we refer:

— the number Q_{ij}, conveniently made homogeneous, of the public vehicles, which are going over each link γ_{ij};

— the number R_{rs}, equal to 1/5 of the demand for traffic by private cars between each couple of vertices A_r and A_s;

— the numbers $M^{(1)}_{rs}$ and $M^{(2)}_{rs}$, properly made homogeneous equal to 1/5 of the vehicles for goods transportation referring to each couple A_r, A_s of vertices; $M^{(1)}_{rs}$ stands for number of vehicles which may go over all links and $M^{(2)}_{rs}$ the number of those which may go only over some of the links.

I must at once say that in the application of such a model it has not been possible to account for the goods traffic because it was carried out before we possessed the relevant data.

We have thus determined the input of our program.

6 Research on minimum duration routes. As a first stage of the program the computer determines the new times of trips for all links of the graph; account being taken of the load due to the public vehicles. One should calculate the time for the link γ_{ij}:

$$t^{(1)}_{ij} = t^{(0)}_{ij} (1 + k_{ij} a_{ij}).$$

The second stage provides for research on the minimum time routes; from each vertex to all the others, according to the duration $t^{(1)}_{ij}$. For the research on these routes [6] the computer operator will proceed along the following process of dynamic programming [7]. Starting from vertex A_i the computer will determine all vertices $A_{j_1}, A_{j_2}, ..., A_{j_{h_1}}$ to be reached by only one step and the pertaining times:

$$t^{(1)}_{ij_1}, ... t^{(1)}_{ij_{h_1}},$$

[6] By using a G.E. 400, kindly allowed by the firm Olivetti-General Electric, it has been ascertained that the determination of the routes of minimum time from one vertex to all the 732 other vertices of the graph of Rome takes 25 seconds.

[7] See e.g. R. Bellman, *Dynamic Programming*, University Press, Princeton, 1957.

Then, those to be reached with at least two steps, A_{j_1}, A_{j_2}, $A_{j_{h_2}}$ and
if in some instances it is possible to get there with one or two steps, he
will decide which of the two routes is more convenient; in order to simplify
the illustration I will say that the times to go from A_i to A_{js} (and the corresponding links) are related to the trips with at least two steps. In a
similar way the computer acts for the times and links referred to the trips
with at least three steps, four steps, etc., until the times and the links
referred to at least $p + 1$ steps coincide with those referred to p steps.

A similar research is then to be made for the minimum time routes
which make use only of links over which go also vehicles unable to make
use of all links. The same operation is to be made for all vertices from
which trips are possible or at least such that on the whole the trips at
their origin surpass a certain value.

As a third stage we must allocate to the routes found above, the
$R_{rs} + M_{rs}^{(1)}$ journeys from A_r to A_s of the cars which may use all links and
the $M_{rs}^{(2)}$ journeys of particular vehicles. After this distribution the links
γ_{ij} will have to bear a further load $b_{ij}^{(1)}$.

The fourth operation is the calculation of the new times of covering
the distances:

$$t_{ij}^{(2)} = t_{ij}^{(0)}\left(1 + k_{ij} \left(a_{ij} + b_{ij}^{(1)}\right) \right).$$

The fifth operation requires the calculation of the new minimum-time
routes according to these new times $t_{ij}^{(2)}$. The sixth operation consists
of attributing a second fifth of the traffic according to the minimum-time
routes of the fourth operation.

The seventh consists of the calculation of the new times of covering
the distances after the supplementary load $b_{ij}^{(2)}$ is allocated to the links
γ_{ij}. And so on until, one fifth after another, all the demand for traffic,
relating to the hour examined, is allocated.

The program of assignment, as one sees, is based on the letting in
one fifth of the traffic at a time. This procedure does not take us to the real
minimization of the total time of transit; but this, as it has been checked
in some empirical experiments, takes us very near the optimal solution,
By inserting the traffic in more than five segments, we would obtain a
better approximation; however the longer computer time would not be
justified, also because a closer approximation to the optimal assignment
does not seem to be desirable since the rule, strictly applied appears
less realistic than the one obtained by allocation of the journeys one
fifth at a time.

Before abandoning this subject of the determination of the routes for the trips, I must add that we have long considered the convenience of giving a certain weight (as for loss of time) to the crossing of nodes, or, more exactly, to the passing from one link to the other (since the nodes on the graph do not at all represent road junctions.)

If γ_{ij} $(j = 1, 2 \ldots, n_i)$ are the links which start at junction i, we thought of calculating the time of passing from a link ending in i to the subsequent one through the relation :

$$\bar{t} \left(\sum_1^{n_i} j \, N_{ij} \right) \bigg/ \left(\sum_1^{n_i} i \, N_{ij}^{(0)} \right)$$

where :

$\bar{t}$ is a constant (in seconds),

N_{ij} is the number of trips utilizing the links γ_{ij},

$N_{ij}^{(0)}$ is the theoretical maximum capacity of the link γ_{ij}.

It would have been very simple to introduce this further element in our model, but it would have made still longer the already very long times necessary to carry out the assignments on the routes. Thus, in the application I shall mention in the next paragraph, we have given up this last refinement of the model which would have had influence essentially on the less loaded links.

7 An application of VIT. I will now state briefly the results and the details of an experiment which, though it relates only to the Rome traffic, certainly interests all cities which have an historic centre to protect and respect. It is an application of necessarily modest dimensions because we had to have recourse for its realization to the kindness of the Olivetti-General Electric who have generously made us a gift of as much as 24 hours on a powerful G.E.400 ; and we could not take too much advantage of this notable generosity.

We have first of all distributed on a graph the traffic of vehicles in the principal peak hour, that is the trips which start between 7 and 8 in the morning.

The distribution has given evidence of the main effect of the network of Rome streets, namely its clear centripetal structure which conveys the vehicles to congest in the most crucial points of the town (Porta Maggiore, Porta S. Giovanni, etc). This defect is particularly serious for the type of traffic that we have considered in the peak hours ; but it is of course a well known defect and there was no need to apply to the VIT for this piece of information. At most one could say that we have thus had a demonstration — not even very significant — of the soundness of the parameters introduced in the model.

This was not the real scope of the application. In fact owing to this defect, it had already been authoritatively stated that it is necessary radically to modify the structure of the street network of Rome, introducing flow lines far from the historic centre.

Of necessity, this is taken into account in the new Town Development Plan when it considers the construction of major external streets away from the heart of the town.

However, there are many who still believe that it is possible to cure the defects of the Rome street network by properly arranging the existing streets, and others are even convinced that a rigid application of the 'Codice della Strada' (Road Code) would be sufficient; or an aggravation of penalties, or a reform in the Codice, or a new one.

To undeceive these optimists, and at times certain optimism is very dangerous, it has been thought of carrying out an interesting experiment with VIT. To this end we have made a distribution of the same trips (departures between seven and eight) on the hypothesis that, maintaining the aggregate number of traffic lanes in both directions of the same thoroughfare, the streets were perfectly equipped; that is to the point that the initial speed should be all equal to the maximum legal speed of 50 km per hour and that there should not be any friction between parallel traffic lanes. Besides, at some points properly chosen, we have also supposed sections of one-way traffic intended to improve the capacity of the whole road system. In short we have supposed that everything was organized according to a perfection unattainable in practice, but essential for our purpose. Also the conditions of constancy in the number of traffic lanes is essential because it reflects the limitations imposed by the respect for old monuments etc. and their conservation in the historic centre and consequently the practical impossibility of effecting massive demolitions in the zones immediately external to the centre.

Anyhow, the introduction of such utopistic structures requires, from the VIT point of view, but few alterations in the parameters of the graph; very easy to apply.

So, I repeat, after having changed in this way the parameters, we have carried out the distribution of the traffic on the graph.

As it was to be expected, the new distribution has not resulted in any great difference from the previous; but it has served to compare the new volumes of traffic on each link with the new values of the corresponding theoretical maximum capacities.

We have thus seen that the links, where the volume of traffic exceeds 75 % of the maximum theoretical capacity, are very many and they include a great number where the volume exceeds 90 % of said capacity.

There is no doubt, as queueing theory tells, that, as soon as 75 % of the theoretical maximum capacity is exceeded, a traffic block occurs caused by the very way, necessarily not uniform, the vehicles reach the corresponding links.

All these links, where, in spite of the supposed new arrangements, the traffic is bound to choke up, show most clearly the validity of the assumption of the Official Town Plan; that is, that the traffic situation in Rome cannot be improved by arranging, even in the most perfect way, the existing streets. Which of course, does not mean that such arrangements are not desirable and to be realized and as soon as possible.

The experiment illustrated above has served also to dispel the myth of the centre. Every time one thinks of alterations to the traffic not only in Rome but for any city with an historic centre, the centre is considered as though the real problems of the traffic were there. It is enough to inspect the graphs we have obtained with VIT to see immediately how scarce, in absolute value, the traffic in the centre is. This traffic, in relative value, is important — as the VIT shows — only because the streets are really narrow and get easily choked. Moral: every intervention in the centre will give results almost irrelevant for the centre itself (unless it consists of a general prohibition for all private vehicles): and, what is worse, it will be entirely useless — if not detrimental — for the really distressing spots in urban traffic.

Traffic, at the point to which Rome has arrived, cannot be cured with 'disc-zones' or with 'rotatory circulation'. The error has been that for too many years one believed in the usefulness of similar provisions and so precious time has been lost playing with instruments which, if at that time produced some benefit, at present are completely useless.

If what we know now about the traffic in Rome had been known in 1960, today matters would be much better. But it is no use crying over spilt milk.

8 The PODS. The other model, which the Istituto di Calcolo delle Probabilità has considered (PODS), has been prepared to predict Rome traffic in 1985. This forecast is indispensable if one wants to avoid the old policy of the dog pursuing the hare, rather than the modern one of the gunner who aims at the future position of the target moving in space at a high speed.

On the other hand, even being optimistic, five years will go before the program of traffic intervention is ready, and another ten years will be taken after that before the significant portion of the work set out by the program may become operative. Therefore, only in 1982 may we see the practical results of the researches on traffic organized by the Town Administration.

In order that these results may be positive, it will first of all be necessary for the plan of traffic changes to take into account, not the traffic of today, but that which we will have at the time the plan comes into operation. For this reason the Municipality has entrusted the Istituto di Calcolo delle Probabilità with the task of preparing a forecasting model of the traffic in 1985.

The idea which has guided the Istituto, when preparing this model, is based on the observation that the traffic is strictly linked with the L.U. and that it is possible to obtain a good forecast of the L.U. in 1985 taking account of the Town Development Plan of Rome and the forecasts (on regional scale) of the National Programme Offices.

To this end the Istituto di Calcolo delle Probabilità has given an explicit form to the existing relationships, in each zone, between the respective L.U. and the number of arrivals or departures (classified by reason and interval of time but not by means, because this last character does not lend itself to be extrapolated). Such relationships are practically expressed by regressions between the number of arrivals (or departures) and the values of the 22 variables of the L.U. of the same zone; in their turn, the functions of the regressions can be approximated by least squares polynomials thus obtaining a pattern of the Rome traffic expressed by a certain number of polynomials in the variables x_i of the L.U. surveys.

The trips have thus been divided in nine groups in accordance with the interval of time in which they started; each one of these groups has been further divided in five sections according to reason (work, school, shopping, return home and others). We will hence have 45 (9×5) least squares polynomials for the departures and as many for the arrivals. The 90 ($= 45 \times 2$) polynomials so obtained, with the necessary corrections, will serve also for the input to the model for traffic in 1985.

It is to be noted that, by increasing the degree of the polynomials, the complication and therefore the cost of the calculations rises very rapidly, whereas the validity of the model (especially for 1985) would receive but very little improvement; it has therefore been decided to adopt polynomials of first degree thus making considerable savings of cost.

Perhaps this is the moment to say explicitly that a forecast has not a strict obligation to correspond to what really happens but only to be consistent with what is presumed. Practically, we all make some forecast when we take any decisions, but we make them in an implicit way and thus run the risk of not being consistent. To forecast in an explicit way allows a certain consistency between what we presume and what we decide upon.

But let us go back to PODS. To indicate the conditions of equilibrium which the 90 linear least squares polynomials which represent the model of the traffic must obey, it is useful to introduce some symbols:

$x_i^{(z)}$: intensity of the i-th character in the z-th zone

$$(i = 1, 2, ..., 22 \, ; \, z = 1, 2, ..., 733)$$

$x_i = \sum_{1}^{733} {}_z \, x_i^{(z)}$: total intensity of the character i-th

${}_p y_{st}^{(z)}$: number of departures, in zone z, concerning reason s and the interval of time t $(s = 1, 2, ..., 5 \, ; \, t = 1, 2, ..., 9)$;

${}_A y_{st}^{(z)}$: number of arrivals, in zone z, for reason s and interval of time t ;

${}_p a_{ist}$: coefficient of x_i in the least square linear polynomial, which gives the departures concerning reason s and the interval of time t (for $i = 0$ one gets a constant).

${}_A a_{ist}$: coefficient of x_i in the least square linear polynomial, which gives the arrivals concerning reasons s and the interval of time t (for $i = 0$ one gets a constant).

By using these symbols, the model is given by :

$$_p y_{st}^{(z)} = \sum_{0}^{22} {}_i \, {}_p a_{ist} x_i^{(z)}$$

$$_A y_{st}^{(z)} = \sum_{0}^{22} {}_i \, {}_A a_{ist}^{(z)}$$

$$\left.\begin{array}{l} z = 1, 2, ..., 733 \\[4pt] s = 1, 2, ..., 5 \\[4pt] t = 1, 2, ..., 9 \end{array}\right\} \quad (3)$$

and the conditions of equilibrium assume the following form :

$$\sum_{0}^{22} {}_{i \, p} a_{ist} x_i = \sum_{0}^{22} {}_i \, {}_A a_{ist} x_i$$

$$\sum_{1}^{5} {}_s \sum_{1}^{9} {}_t \, {}_p a_{ist} = \sum_{1}^{5} {}_s \sum_{1}^{9} {}_t \, {}_A a_{ist} \quad (4)$$

For the different values of s and t, the first of the relations (4) gives 45 conditions which express how, for fixed reason and interval of time, the departures are as many as the arrivals; while the second, for the different values of i gives 23 relations which express how, in each of the 733 Zones the departures and the arrivals, in the 24 hours, are of equal number.

The coupling of said departures and arrivals to form the origin and the destination of the same journeys is obtainable through a suitable procedure which I will not present in detail now.

The second step consisted in the construction of L.U. in 1985. To this end, an accurate study has been made along three directions (economic, demographic and urban) which however have never been considered separately one from the other (ignoring, that is to say, their reciprocal entireness) but dealt with, all the three *pari-passu*. This vast research has permitted a first sub-division of the activities in the municipal territory and has led to the determination of the totals of the 22 variables of the L.U. These totals are shown in the table on page 97 with the present figures. With all due consideration, these totals have been placed on the 733 zones thus obtaining the L.U. for 1985.

The model of traffic for 1964 cannot be applied — without proper adjustments — to 1985 both because the increase of motoring (as number of cars per 100 inhabitants) implies a certain increase in traffic, and because the very structure of the town will be changed.

The increase of traffic due to more extensive motoring bears essentially on trips for shopping, on those for other reasons and, in consequence, on those for return home.

On the basis of the experience of American cities, such increase has been introduced by augmenting by 30 % the coefficients which in the current model appear in the equations concerning the trips for shopping and those for other reasons; these supplementary trips have been largely compensated with the return trips home of the appropriate intervals of time.

Having introduced these adjustments, we have then taken into account the different structure of the town, introducing the necessary adjustments to satisfy the conditions of equilibrium, on the basis of which the number of departures must be equal to those of arrivals for the same reason and for the same interval of time. In this simple adjustment care has always been taken to re-establish equilibrium at the level of the greater of the two initial numbers (and this on the basis of the well known observation that in the very large majority of cases, forecasts turn out to be underestimates).

Similar adjustments have been made for the model of goods transportation in which, however, the coefficients of the current model have all been previously increased by 10 %, so as to take into account the increase in average consumption per individual.

Going back to persons trips, I must add that with the model thus obtained, we have calculated zone by zone the number of arrivals and departures for each reason and for each interval of time. The aggregate number of journeys in the 24 hours has amounted to 6 201 429.

Variables	Totals present	in 1985
x_1 = Population: head of family indept.	58 912	109 384
x_2 = Population: head of family subordinate	908 467	1 498 282
x_3 = Population: head of family other position	1 171 293	2 171 912
x_4 = People in: industry	190 294	382 648
x_5 = People in: commerce	139 642	252 869
x_6 = People in: transport	79 689	122 705
x_7 = People in: banking	53 144	112 860
x_8 = People in: pub. admin.	109 657	162 445
x_9 = Teachers	29 968	64 927
x_{10} = Schools: infant (pupils)	54 726	186 373
x_{11} = Schools: primary (pupils)	181 368	288 353
x_{12} = Schools: grammar (students)	91 293	171 614
x_{13} = Schools: high (students)	76 719	174 141
x_{14} = Schools: university (students)	52 230	86 484
x_{15} = Licences (wholesale)	1 893	3 099
x_{16} = Licences (retail-food)	40 125	72 156
x_{17} = Licences (retail-non food)	40 098	81 344
x_{18} = Licences (supermarkets)	27	279
x_{19} = Licences (cinemas etc.)	467	1 082
x_{20} = Hospitals (n. of beds)	31 125	51 035
x_{21} = Ambulatories	507	958
x_{22} = Stadium & gymnasium (index freq.)	2 095	4 189

Trips tabulated according to reason and time intervals as at 1964 – persons

REASON	TIME INTERVALS									TOTAL
	2.01-7.00	7.01-8.00	8.01-12.30	12.31-13.30	13.31-16.30	16.31-17.30	17.31-19.00	19.01-20.00	20.01-2.00	
Work	240 525	268 527	141 422	18 037	199 584	28 332	13 574	5 066	6 892	921 959
School	8 153	130 481	78 629	29 388	24 211	2 730	4 144	1 057	---	278 793
Shopping	2 061	5 021	107 520	707	11 032	10 650	9 451	1 023	---	147 465
Return home	3 321	3 801	280 678	266 983	244 282	137 555	184 336	195 409	156 946	1 453 311
Other reason	7 095	26 309	97 080	9 750	61 864	32 240	29 390	11 384	16 798	291 910
TOTAL	261 155	434 139	705 329	324 865	520 973	211 507	240 895	213 939	180 636	3 093 438

Trips tabulated according to reason and time intervals as at 1985 — persons in percent of the corresponding values of 1964

TIME INTERVALS

REASON	2.01-7.00	7.01-8.00	8.01-12.30	12.31-13.30	13.31-16.30	16.31-17.30	17.31-19.00	19.01-20.00	20.01-2.00	
Work	167·9	181·6	176·6	171·4	184·1	185·4	172·0	181·2	172·0	177·5
School	172·4	182·3	192·3	209·0	196·3	172·7	128·2	134·4	— —	187·8
Shopping	187·3	233·8	253·7	283·6	405·7	425·8	407·2	453·2	— —	287·2
Return home	169·7	192·5	202·6	211·4	185·5	199·8	188·2	188·9	188·3	196·0
Other reason	227·0	259·4	264·3	289·5	272·0	256·7	266·3	277·9	235·8	263·7
	169·8	187·3	212·5	211·4	200·4	217·5	204·4	194·4	192·1	200·5

Trips tabulated according to reason and time intervals as at 1985 — persons

REASON	TIME INTERVALS									TOTAL
	2.01-7.00	7.01-8.00	8.01-12.30	12.31-13.30	13.31-16.30	16.31-17.30	17.31-19.00	19.01-20.00	20.01-2.00	
Work	403 752	487 652	249 764	30 909	367 383	52 537	23 351	9 178	11 851	1 636 377
School	14 053	237 912	151 186	61 421	47 521	4 716	5 312	1 421	— —	523 542
Shopping	3 860	11 738	272 748	2 005	44 756	45 343	38 489	4 636	— —	423 575
Return home	5 637	7 317	568 771	564 336	415 959	274 767	346 767	369 002	295 474	2 848 205
Other reason	16 109	68 245	256 630	28 228	168 239	82 764	78 264	31 638	39 613	769 730
TOTAL	443 411	812 864	1 499 099	686 899	1 043 858	460 127	492 358	415 875	346 938	6 201 429

Trips of vehicles for goods transportation at
1964 and 1985 per time interval

Time Intervals	(a) 1964	(b) 1985	$\frac{(b)}{(a)} 100$
2.01 - 7.00	19 271	36 132	187·5
7.01 - 8.00	18 373	36 500	198·7
8.01 - 12.30	85 033	168 640	198·3
12.31 - 13.30	12 661	24 259	191·6
13.31 - 16.30	26 355	50 304	190·9
16.31 - 17.30	10 016	20 124	200·9
17.31 - 19.00	10 129	20 879	206·1
19.01 - 20.00	4 775	9 561	200·2
20.01 - 2.00	4 522	7 379	163·18
	191 135	373 778	195·6

APPENDIX BY DR. GORI

The program in FORTRAN Language starts with the acceptance, from a previously loaded tape, of the data of the matix corresponding to the graph.

This tape will also be used to fix the situation at the end of each cycle, thus allowing interruption at any moment and the subsequent resumption from the interrupted cycle.

The second step of the program is the input from another tape of the data concerning the origins, destinations, and number of vehicles interested in the route. A switch in the program allows the modifications which permit taking account of public vehicles to be obtained immediately. In the following cycles, one obtains the prints of the routes and of the subsequent modifications. At the start the definition of some variables is required, in this order:

N   = number of links
IN   = 99 ... 9 (infinite)
L   = number of nodes
NO   = number of origins
LIC   = limits of the cycles
NIC   = number of cycles from which to start
ISW1 = 1 with public vehicles
        0 without public vehicles
ISW2 = 1 without public vehicles
        0 with public vehicles or for resumption
ORIGN = origin
DESTN = destination
PASGI = passages
PERCR = route
SPIGL = link
IDA   = from
IA   = to
CARIC = load
TPRCR = time of covering the distance
CICLO = cycle

descriptive alphabetical constants

Minimum configuration required: 8 K core plus backing store, two tapes and a console.

The first six dimensioned variables correspond to the indexes j and i, and to the elements of the four matrices which show the values k_{ij} the numbers of public vehicles the $t^{(N1)}_{ij}$ and $t^{(0)}_{ij}$. The value of L S is arbitrary and may be taken on the basis of the presumable maximum numbers of nodes which the various routes may have.

Specifications concerning the preparation of the tapes, data and procedures of operations may be had directly from the Istituto di Calcolo delle Probabilità in the Rome University.

```
DIMENSION IJ (N), II (N), IK (N), IM (N), IT (N), ITI (N), IALFA (L), IC (L)
            IDS (LS), LD (L)
ACCEPT 99, N, IN, L, NO, LIC, NIC, ISW1, ISW2, ORIGN, DESTN,
            PASGI, PERCR, SPIGL, IDA, IA, CARIC, TPRCR, CICLO
FORWARD TAPE 1,1
FORWARD TAPE 2,2
J = 0
M = 0
IF (NIC) 101, 100, 101
101 NN = NIC * N
FORWARD TAPE 1, NN
100 DO 1 I = 1, N
READ INPUT TAPE 1, 99, IJ (I), II (I), IK (I), IM (I), IT (I), ITI (I)
IF (IJ (I) – J) 1, 1, 21
21 J = IJ (I)
M = M + 1
IC (M) = I
1 CONTINUE
IF (ISW1) 22, 23, 22
22 NI = 0
TYPE 99, CICLO, NI
GO TO 18
23 IF (ISW2) 31, 32, 31
31 DO 2 I = 1, N
2 IM (I) = 0
32 NI = NIC
20 IO = 0
TYPE 99, CICLO, NI
17 READ INPUT TAPE 2, 99, JO, ND
ID = 0
IO = IO + 1
DO 3 I = 1, L
```

```
IALFA (I) = IN
3LD (I) = JO
IALFA (JO) = 0
8IBETA = 0
M = 1
27 IF (IALFA (II (M)) − IN) 4, 5, 4
4IS = IALFA (II (M)) + II (M)
IF (IALFA (IJ (M)) − IS) 5, 5, 7
7IALFA (IJ (M)) = IS
LD (IJ (M)) = II (M)
IBETA = 1
5M = M + 1
IF (M − N) 27, 27, 6
6IF (IBETA) 8, 9, 8
9 IF (SENSE SWITCH 2) 66, 65
66 TYPE 99, IDA, IA, TPRCR
DO 90 I = 1, L
90 TYPE 99, JO, I, IALFA (I)
65 READ INPUT TAPE 2, 99, I, NM
J = LS (*)
ID = ID + 1
14M = IC (I)
15 IF (II (M) − LD (I)) 10, 11, 10
11 IM (M) = IM (M) + NM
IDS (J) = I
J = J − 1
IF (LD (I) − JO) 12, 13, 12
12I = LD (I)
GO TO 14
10M = M + 1
GO TO 15
13IDS (J) = JO
TYPE 99, ORIGN, JO, DESTN, IDS (LS), PASGI, NN
TYPE 99, PERCR
DO 26 IS = J, LS (*)
26 TYPE 99, IDS (IS)
IF (ID − ND) 65, 16, 16
```

(*) See comment.

```
16 IF (IO — NO) 17, 18, 18
18 IF (SENSE SWITCH 3) 69, 70
69 TYPE 99, SPIGL, IDA, IA, CARIC, TPRCR
70 DO 33 I = 1, N
IT (I) = ITI (I) * (1 + IK (I) * IM (I))
IF (SENSE SWITCH 3) 19, 33
19 TYPE 99, II (I), IJ (I), IM (I), IT (I) ·
33 CONTINUE
NI = NI + 1
BACKWARD TAPE 2, 0
DO 30 I = 1, N
30 WRITE OUTPUT TAPE 1, 99, IJ (I), II (I), IK (I), IM (I), IT (I), ITI (I)
29 IF (NI — LIC) 20, 20, 25
25 STOP
```

AIR TRAFFIC CONTROL – MODELS AND MYTHS

P. C. HAINES

CONTENTS

1 Introduction

1.1 This paper discusses the need for, the use and the mis-use of, modelling techniques in the analysis and design of air traffic control systems.

2 Principles of air traffic control

2.1 The expressed aims of air traffic control (A T C) are the achievement of 'a safe, orderly and expeditious flow of air traffic'. The current and foreseeable high level of capital investment in ground and airborne equipment makes it generally accepted that there must be a further objective – economy of operation.

2.2 Over the years, a complex and world wide A T C organization has been built up, based upon a concept of 'controlled airspace' – i.e. a defined volume of airspace under the jurisdiction of an A T C authority. Such controlled airspaces may be allocated, in whole or in part, for the exclusive use of particular aircraft. The map at Fig. 1 (page 123) shows some of the controlled airspace in the United Kingdom, comprising airways which connect with Terminal Areas (TM A) around airports whence air traffic is fed into or from the airways.

2.3 In controlled airspace, collision avoidance is achieved by ensuring that aircraft do not infringe given Separation Minima, which stipulate that, in the interests of safety, aircraft must be separated by designated track, by time or by height, or, additionally in the TM A, by lateral displacement. Two different types of control technique are used –

one of a strategic or procedural nature, based upon statement of aircraft intention updated by aircraft position reports, and one of a tactical nature, based upon radar-derived information. Under certain circumstances, these two types of control may be combined. When using only the procedural technique, the performance necessitates the use of large separation criteria, thus leading to inefficient use of the available airspace. The radar-based technique which provides frequent and accurate information about aircraft plan position, permits of closer aircraft spacing but leads to significant data-handling and processing problems. In general, radar still does not provide accurate information about aircraft height, and therefore the third dimension, the 'z' axis, is as yet not fully exploited.

2.4 It will be seen from the map that airways are defined by Reporting Points. Navigational aids are sited at these Reporting Points in order that aircraft may establish their position reasonably accurately at the critical time when they need to report their position to the control organization. Thus, the airways and the Reporting Points provide a geographical frame of reference for the procedural type of control system. Control is exercised by collating aircraft position reports with reference to the reporting points and allocating appropriate heights, and/or delaying aircraft in such a manner that flight paths do not conflict.

2.5 The procedural A T C technique, based on the position reports and upon estimated time of arrival at fixed reporting points, therefore introduces discrete steps into a continuous process and control is achieved, in effect, by modelling the system. By contrast, the tactical control technique based upon radar-derived information updated every few seconds at each sweep of the radar, is more nearly a continuous process.

3 Development of A T C organization

3.1 The history of air traffic control is relatively short. The first steps to introduce effective control systems were taken in the United States in the early 1930's. Prior to the second world war, no serious endeavour was made to rationalize the growth and organization of air traffic control. In 1945, an attempt was made to remedy this situation and to co-ordinate development through the Provisional International Civil Aviation Organization. However, international organizations inevitably move slowly, and system development has in fact proceeded on a largely piecemeal basis, with additional controllers, equipment and procedures being introduced from time to time to relieve strain as it has become apparent. As controllers or control sectors have become overloaded, the airspaces have been further subdivided between more and more controllers. More and more tactical procedures have been devised requiring bigger and better radars and still more controllers to operate them. In the busier Air Traffic Control Centres this process has now reached the point of diminishing returns, where the useful capacity of each controller is being reduced by the growing need for liaison and co-ordination.

3.2 For the first time, it is now being recognised that it is essential to examine the performance of A T C systems as a whole and to match the capacities of the various units which together comprise the total systems. In particular, it is becoming evident that greater use must be made of the potential conferred upon aircraft, with the more general introduction of airborne computers, to navigate in three dimensions. Overall it is hoped to achieve an optimum or near optimum balance between airborne navigation capability, the use of ground-based data acquisition systems, data processing and display systems, and, at the same time to relieve the controller of all other than essential judgement and decision processes.

4 Systems analysis

4.1 It is useful to examine A T C from a broad Operational Research point of view.

4.2 **Network flow system.** An A T C system may be considered as a 'network flow system', characterized by a static 'environment', the route structure, through which individual 'items', the aircraft, are processed according to specified rules. The 'environment' has a finite capacity due, amongst other factors, to the imposition of A T C separation standards and to the physical dimensions of the airways. Such limitations lead to queues of 'items' being formed at one or more places within the environment, for example, in holding stacks for inbound, and at runways for outbound aircraft, and to the necessity of re-routeing some 'items' in an attempt to obtain an improved movement rate. In the particular case of A T C, re-routeing is taken in its wider sense to include the allocation of an alternative cruising level, a change to a parallel track, interruption of a flight profile by stopping-off a climb or descent, as well as the allocation of an alternative route. Movement of the 'items', in other words, the traffic flow, is subject to 'constraints' which may be dependent upon the identities and states of the individual 'items' as well as upon the 'environment'. Such 'constraints' take the form of A T C rules and regulations, and the physical limitations of individual aircraft, such as restrictions on the range of acceptable cruising levels, the rates of climb and descent, and the navigational capability.

4.3 **Cybernetic system.** Basically this constitutes a complex Cybernetic System in which a 'decision making element', the controller, receives information concerning the environment and items within the environment and then exercises a 'control action' over the latter with the express purpose of achieving a particular objective; in this case to provide for an expeditious flow of traffic, as closely as possible in conformity with the expressed wishes of the aircraft, whilst maintaining safety by ensuring that potential conflicts between aircraft are detected and resolved. Such 'control action' takes place in the presence of 'external agents' which can modify or affect the system independently of the 'decision making element'. Included in these 'external agents' are meteorological factors such as wind, temperature and pressure, errors in the navigation of the aircraft and errors in the ATC picture of the actual traffic situation.

4.4 Summarising, an ATC system has :-

    (a) A static 'Environment' :- the route structure

    (b) 'Items' flowing through the environment :- the aircraft

    (c) 'Constraints' on the items :- ATC rules and regulations, physical limitations of the system and the aircraft

    (d) A 'Decision making element' :- the Air Traffic Control Officer

    (e) A general objective :- a safe and expeditious flow of traffic

    (f) 'External Agents' :- meteorological conditions and errors.

4.5 How can such a system be evaluated? Can experimentation with the real system produce the required information or is it necessary to construct a model? If so, what sort of model — a physical working model, a set of mathematical equations or a written description of the system expressed in logical terms?

4.6 In general, there are three ways of evaluating ATC system performance :-

    (a) Experimentation with the real system

    (b) Mathematical analysis

    (c) Experimentation with a model — known technically as Simulation.

5 Evaluation of an ATC system

Experimentation with the real system

5.1 In many cases experimentation with the real system is not possible because the alternative solutions to be tested involve irrevocable and mutually exclusive changes in the environment, for example the siting of the third London airport. Although changes in rules and procedures could be considered by this technique, experimentation could often result in disruption of the system under study and be costly in time and money when applied to complex situations. The pertinent features of a system are not always subject to control in the actual system and it is not possible to make experimental studies of the effect of introducing, say, a new item of physical performance surpassing that of any existing item, for example the introduction of supersonic aircraft into present systems. Moreover, experiments with real A T C systems may involve danger to life and property which cannot be justified.

Mathematical analysis

5.2 By expressing the behaviour of the actual system in mathematical terms, various analytical or ordinary mathematical methods may be applied directly to investigate the effect of alterations to both the environment and the constraints. Yet mathematical analysis of complex systems is often impossible, either because suitable analytical methods have not so far been developed, or because their application would take too long. In general an A T C system is complex, involving many variables and features which cannot be expressed in simple mathematical terms, and which by the very nature of the problem cannot be subdivided into simpler secondary problems which can be studied analytically.

Experimentation with a model

5.3 The remaining possibility is that of simulation, which involves the study of the behaviour of a Model, either physical or logical in nature, of the real-life system and of experimenting with the model very much in the way that one would wish to be able to experiment with the actual system. It has the advantage of being able to cope with problems which are mathematically intractable and which resist solution by analytical methods, at the same time saving the potentially high cost, dangers and difficulties of experimenting with the real system incorporating facilities which, whilst foreseeable and possibly capable of precise definition, are not yet available in the real system.

5.4 In practice, simulation techniques may be divided into two distinct fields, Operational Gaming and Arithmetical Simulation.

5.5 *Operational Gaming.* Operational Gaming is a term to describe simulation techniques in which the reaction of human participants involved in the operation of the system are not simulated artificially. In other words, no attempt is made to 'model' human behaviour; the human operators (controllers and pilots) participate in the experiments, carrying out their functions in the same way as they would in the real system. In the A T C field this form of simulation is referred to as Real-Time Simulation, since, in general, it takes the same time to experiment with the model as with the real system because the time dimension is retained in an unmodelled form. Some time-saving may be obtained, however, as none is wasted waiting for conditions to occur which may be important but only happen occasionally in real-life, for example, poor visibility.

5.6 The process consists of generating an artificial traffic sample by manual or computer methods and presenting the information describing the resultant traffic situation to the human operators for maintaining a safe and expeditious flow of traffic through the model. As the simulation proceeds, the 'traffic flow' is modified as necessary by instructions from the controllers in accordance with the rules and regulations selected for the particular experiment. Actual operating conditions are reproduced as nearly as possible, thus enabling maximum realism to be introduced.

5.7 However, it must be stated that one of the myths not yet fully exploded is that Real-Time Simulation will solve all future problems. Heavy capital investment has been made in equipment, but, whilst ideally suited for study and resolution of ergonomic problems, Real-Time Simulation suffers many disadvantages in regard to the broader problem of large-scale systems analysis in that :-

(a) The process is slow since the time dimension is not simulated, and the accumulation of sufficient information from which to deduce statistically significant results is a lengthy procedure.

(b) The results, consequently, are normally few and usually influenced by many subjective views.

(c) Accordingly, comparison between experimental results may be invalidated by human variation from exercise to exercise.

(d) Special and usually expensive equipment is required.

(e) The proportion of a large system capable of investigation in any one exercise is necessarily limited by the available simulation facilities.

(f) It is a major problem to collect together the large number of qualified A T C personnel.

(g) Later repetition of an exercise under controlled experimental conditions is practically impossible.

5.8 Nevertheless, operational gaming has made important contributions when human reaction to environmental conditions is itself the subject of investigation, and also when human behaviour cannot be described sufficiently well in logical terms to permit the use of other techniques.

5.9 *Arithmetic Simulation.* The disadvantage of operational gaming can be largely overcome by eliminating the human factor and simulating the fourth dimension — time. This is what happens in the Arithmetical Simulation method where the complete system, including the behaviour of human participants, is expressed in mathematical or logical terms. The replacement of human processes by purely logical mechanisms enables time to be simulated by treating it as a simple mathematical parameter. As the whole A T C system is translated into logical and arithmetic terms, use can be made of high speed digital computers and the simulation process may be made to operate many times faster than real-time. In this way it is possible to examine a greater range of situations and to obtain statistically viable results more quickly.

5.10 The continuous nature of the real system is transformed by arithmetic simulation into a discontinuous model. This presents no significant problem as ATC itself considers the environment at discrete points, known as reporting points, thus effecting a similar, though not identical, transformation. The model may be treated in one of two ways. In the first, known as Unit Time Scan Simulation, simulated time is advanced in constant, discrete increments, corresponding for example to the period of rotation of a radar head. The condition of the system is examined after each increment and all operations or decisions deemed necessary are carried out before the time is advanced further. The method is of value when the system to be examined is one of continuous change or else involves many interacting events occurring in rapid succession or with known periodicity. However, this is not always the case and if the model has to be examined many times before any important changes do, in fact, occur, the unit time scan simulation technique is clearly wasteful of computer time.

5.11 If the real-life situation is predictable between events, the model need be examined, or scanned, only when an event significant in the context of the simulation actually occurs. Under these circumstances simulated time may be advanced on the completion of each event to the time at which the next significant event occurs. This gives rise to the second method, known as 'Event to Event' Simulation where time is advanced by variable increments. Generally, in an ATC system, an aircraft must report to ground control when it passes over specified geographical points known as reporting points which are variable distances apart, dependent upon the environment. Thus an 'Event' occurs each time an aircraft reports, but the majority of these reports are routine, and require no action to be taken by the controller other than the recording of information, and do not affect the state of the system. However, at certain reporting points the controller must examine the system to ensure that the aircraft remains on a conflict-free path over a specified distance. This may occur on the transfer of control of the aircraft from one unit of ATC ground control to the next, or when ATC detects that its estimate of the aircraft position is in error. At these points the events are 'Critical' and can alter the state of the simulation. The simulation technique, which has been extensively developed and applied by General Precision Systems (GPS) to problems in the field of ATC, automatically advances simulated time from one 'critical' event to the next, and is known as 'Critical Event Simulation'.

6 The modelling of an ATC system by critical event simulation

Model specification

6.1 The first step in the modelling is to transform the real ATC system which is to be investigated into the logical terms forming the model. The resultant model of the system will obviously depend upon the exact purpose of the investigation, which must be precisely defined before any serious attempt at simulation is made. Phase one in the planning of a simulation project thus consists of detailed discussions between the clients and the ATC experts of the study team to define the exact objectives of the investigation, which at the outset are often not clearly defined. The real ATC system is then examined in detail by operational and mathematical analysts in order to extract the salient features in order to permit the development of the *simplest* possible model which will satisfy the objectives. Phases two and three of the investigation can be subdivided under the following headings :-

(a) the environment

(b) the constraints

(c) the decision logic

(d) the time element

(e) the traffic sample.

6.2 *The environment.* The environment comprises a network of fixed airways of stated width about a series of straight lines joining specified geographical points, and subdivided in the vertical plane into a number of flight levels according to certain rules. The airspace itself is partitioned into sectors, each of which is under the authority of a discrete unit of the ATC ground organization.

6.3 In the simulation model the environment is defined by the geographical co-ordinates (latitude and longitude) of all reporting points, over which it is obligatory for aircraft to report to the appropriate ground control. These include such points as the intersection of two or more airways, navigational beacons, and the points at which airways cross sector boundaries. Further amplification of the environment may be necessary in the form of co-ordinates of points which are not reporting points, but are expected to be of importance in the experiments to be conducted on the model. The environment at this stage has been transformed from a continuous medium into a discrete number of disconnected points. A simulated route is defined by a list of these points, identified numerically and ordered in such a way that the first member in the list is the point of entry for the route into the simulated environment, the second member is the next point on the route, and so on, until the point of exit.

6.4 If the model is to be as general as possible, the simulated environment must be capable of modification without the consequent need to change the logical structure of the model itself. For this reason the co-ordinates of the various points and the route information are specified as data to be input to the model.

6.5 *Constraints.* The standards of lateral, longitudinal and vertical separation, together with the limitations of availability and extent of radar coverage, the maximum delay which can be tolerated by the aircraft, the flight levels available to aircraft proceeding in a specified direction, for example, are also introduced into the simulation model in the form of input data so that they may be readily varied. However, the method of application of these constraints forms an integral part of the model logic and as such cannot be specified in terms of input data.

6.6 *Decision logic.* In the real system, human intervention provides the controlling mechanism which regulates the flow of traffic by the application of ATC rules and regulations. Selection between the many rules which may be applicable in a given situation, and the consequential decision, are left finally to the controller's discretion. The satisfactory transformation of these human decision processes into logical terms is crucial to success and makes severe demands upon operational expertise and capability for logical analysis. Evidently the transformation can only be achieved providing the decisions themselves are logical and the rules governing such decisions are known or can be deduced from a study of the system. In practice it is found that even simple ATC rules can give rise to complex logical mechanisms and that the weighting given by a controller to factors involved in a decision will depend on his own experience. Such human variations, coupled with the fact that the simulation model will simplify the decision process, must in absolute terms affect the quantitative results obtained from the simulation study but need not invalidate comparison of alternative systems, provided that the salient points of the system are retained.

6.7 Decision logic is expressed in Boolean algebra terms, consisting essentially of a network of questions and actions, the path through which depends on the 'true' or 'false' nature of the answers to successive questions. As an example, consider a search for potential conflict between two aircraft:

Question 1 : Is the longitudinal separation equal to or greater than the specified minimum?

Yes, i.e. true, then no conflict;
No, i.e. false, then —

Question 2 : Is the vertical separation equal to or greater than the specified minimum?

Yes, i.e. true, then no conflict
No, i.e. false, then —

Question 3 : Is the lateral separation equal to or greater than the specified minimum?

Yes, i.e. true, then no conflict;
No, i.e. false, then a potential conflict exists.

6.8 *Time.* Control of aircraft and the prediction of potential conflicts by A T C is based on the information received by A T C from the aircraft reports and from A T C's own estimates of aircraft performance. Conclusions drawn from this information are subject to distortion due to various factors, particularly meteorological conditions, and therefore do not give a true picture of the traffic situation. Given a requirement for a *realistic* model it is therefore necessary to include facilities for simulating both the *actual* traffic situation and the situation as it is seen, or is estimated, by A T C. Under these circumstances, an aircraft would be characterized at each point along its route by two time parameters; the actual time of arrival (A T A) and the estimated time of arrival (E T A). But care has to be exercised in determining whether a Critical Event occurs at A T A or E T A, although in general this would depend on the activity in question.

6.9 *Traffic sample.* In a real system aircraft positions are known to A T C only by position reports given at discrete intervals of time or by echoes displayed on a radar screen and updated at regular intervals of, say, 10 seconds. Control of the aircraft is executed using both this information and knowledge of the intention of the aircraft obtained from filed flight plans and data transferred from other A T C units. Parameters required to produce this information and characterize the path of an aircraft through the system include specification of the origin, destination, scheduled time of take-off, range of acceptable cruising levels, aircraft performance figures, and standard of navigational capability. For input into the simulation these parameters must be coded in a suitable numerical form.

Programming

6.10 Once the logic of the simulation model has been specified, phase four of the investigation, the transformation of the model into a computer program, is initiated. Programming codes specially designed for simulation are available. However, for either or both technical and economic reasons, these codes have been found to have disadvantages for A T C simulation, possibly because they were developed for equally specific tasks of a different nature. G P S has therefore developed a set of procedures, in a high-level programming language, to perform the various 'housekeeping' tasks required in A T C simulation, and, in particular, to facilitate the handling of essential data sets or lists and to economize on storage allocation.

6.11 To provide a model of maximum versatility and minimum running costs, the A T C simulation programs are normally divided into three separate and distinct parts:

(a) Data Generation Program

(b) Main Simulation Program

(c) Analysis Program.

6.12 Programs are written in a universal high-level language in order that they may be easily transferred from one computer to another, as it necessary when programs are being developed for final production running on a client's own machine to which access for development work either is not available or would involve economic problems. This may be less efficient in storage space and running time than using machine codes but, with programs of such complexity, it would be virtually impossible to write and debug a machine code program within a realistic time scale.

6.13 As far as possible, programs are 'modular' in construction, consisting of a number of distinct sub-programs, sub-routines, or procedures, each representing a specific part of the logic. For example, the allocation of routes dependent on origin and destination, conflict prediction, conflict resolution, various activities associated with critical events and output of results are each written as separate procedures and are called up as required, by the main body of each program. In this way routines may be individually removed, reorganized or rewritten as required to represent any particular ATC system, without disturbing the general framework of the model. This facility enables a wide variety of ATC systems to be simulated on the same model with the minimum of re-programming and debugging.

6.14 *Data Generation Program.* The Data Generation Program prepares the data required for the simulation. It accepts a basic traffic sample consisting of a list of aircraft, with information such as origin, destination, aircraft type and requested cruising level, which are to be processed through the simulated area within a specified time period. Using this data in conjunction with a knowledge of the route structure, obtained from a prior input of parameters defining the particular environment to be simulated, each aircraft is allocated the appropriate route with available alternatives to be used should its first choice become unavailable due to saturation. Nominal performance figures for aircraft of different type at various heights or flight levels are found from tables stores within the computer. To introduce a greater degree of realism into the model the effects of variations in these nominal figures due to factors such as the aircraft loading, meteorological conditions and general variation between individual aircraft are taken into account by random selection of factors from known or assumed variability distributions. Thus, for example, a 'disturbance' is applied to nominal speed to produce a resultant 'actual' speed used in the calculation of Actual Times of Arrival (ATA). By applying similar 'disturbance' to the 'actual' performance figures, simulated ATC estimates are obtained. This introduces a realistic difference between the 'actual' traffic situation and the situation as seen by ATC, such as will always be present in the real environment. Further parameters necessary to characterize aircraft progress through the system may be disturbed by factors drawn at random from predetermined distributions; for example, the actual time of departure from the origin is obtained by disturbing the scheduled time in a suitable manner.

6.15 The process of disturbing the traffic sample and generating the necessary flight information, 'actual' and 'estimated', is repeated for all aircraft in the sample, which are then sorted into chronological order of initial 'offertime' to the simulated area and 'dumped' on to magnetic tape. The whole process is then repeated until the required number of iterations of the traffic sample, with different sets of random factors, is obtained. The data generation output tape consisting of the disturbed traffic samples, preceeded by essential environmental information, such as distances between reporting points, provides the necessary input to the Main Simulation Program.

6.16 *Main Simulation Program.* The Main Simulation Program is designed to process the aircraft through the simulated environment according to specified A T C rules and regulations using the 'Critical Event' form of arithmetic simulation. Aircraft are transferred, one at a time, from the ordered data generation output tape into an 'offering buffer' where they remain 'static' until the simulated time is advanced to the appropriate offertime when the aircraft leaves the buffer and becomes 'active' in the context of the simulation.

6.17 Parameters describing aircraft in the simulated complex may be classified according to their 'dynamic' or 'static' nature. Static information associated with an aircraft within the simulated environment, such as its performance category, requested cruising level, requested and alternative routes, origin and destination, is retained in an 'Active Aircraft' array or set, and it is the address of the aircraft within this set which serves to identify it uniquely throughout the simulation process. Dynamic information, which is dependent upon aircraft position in the system, and/or time is stored in lists or sets associated with each environmental point and known as 'Route Point Sets'. These are processed by means of special dynamic storage routines designed to minimize the storage capacity involved by absorbing large aircraft density fluctuations within the simulated area, by varying, as necessary the size of individual Route Point sets at the expense or advantage of a common reserve set. Total storage for dynamic information can therefore be expressed as a function of the mean traffic density instead of the peak density thus saving considerable computer space. Each 'Route Point Set' must contain sufficient information to enable possible conflicts between aircraft to be detected and may also hold additional information to make the simulation process more efficient. Critical times, the times at which critical events are forecast to occur, are held in a 'Time-Set' together with a note of the relevant activity, the identification of the aircraft involved, and a parameter specifying the position in the environment at which the activity takes place. Examples of the type of activity which may be expected in a general ATC system are 'take-off' activity, 'warning' activity, where an aircraft is 'warned' to an ATC ground control unit prior to its entry into the associated controlled airspace, 'amendment' activity where ATC estimates are updated and a reclearance obtained on the basis of these new estimates, and 'landing' activity.

6.18 The simulation proceeds by a process of searching the Time-Set to determine the event with the earliest critical time, carrying out the necessary activity, updating the Time-Set in respect of the aircraft involved and searching once more for the next critical event and so repeating the process. Generally in an investigation into an ATC system the penalties incurred by individual aircraft are not of direct interest, the system being evaluated on the basis of probability of penalty, average and overall penalties. It can therefore be assumed that aircraft are independent in the sense that an activity carried out for one aircraft does not affect any other aircraft in the system, at least until the next critical event. An aircraft can thus be considered 'dormant' during the time interval between its own critical events.

6.19 At the conclusion of each activity the simulation program outputs, on magnetic tape, the raw results and other data which is essential for system evaluation. For example, when an aircraft is subjected to a change in flight path due to a predicted conflict, information such as the time and position of the aircraft when the potential conflict was detected, the other aircraft involved in the conflict and the avoiding action taken, will be output.

6.20 *Analysis Program.* The Analysis Program accepts the detailed history of the system, recorded during the running of the simulation program, and performs a data processing operation, sorting this information and arranging it in a more digestible form. Typical output will include assessment of the ATC constraints imposed on aircraft, route loadings, number of conflicts predicted and resolved and the demand for given categories of ATC workload. Results may take the form of average and total values, histograms, distributions, frequencies etc. For example:-

(a) The delay imposed on various types of aircraft expressed as average and total value, and probabilities of exceeding given amounts of delay over specified time periods.

(b) The frequency of level change and the percentage of time spent at non-optimum cruising levels.

(c) The percentage of time during which the various workloads, queue lengths, etc. exceed given values.

(d) The distribution of the duration of radar surveillance.

6.21 In theory, the data should be tabulated within the computer and partially analyzed during the main simulation run so that the simulation process can be continued using the various iterations of the basic traffic sample until the results reach the required statistical significance levels, where applicable. However, this is usually impossible because of storage limitations and it is therefore essential to be able to restart the main simulation program from the detailed 'state of play' of the system reached at the end of a simulation run. This may be done by 'dumping' the current parameter values on to a magnetic tape which can subsequently be used to initialize the simulation program at the exact point at which it was previously stopped, should this be necessary.

6.22 The sub-dividing of the simulation into three distinct programs enables :-

(a) The simulation to be repeated without the expense of rerunning the data generation program if the changes to be introduced do not affect either the traffic sample or the route structure, for example, a reduction in separation minima or an increase in the navigational capacity of the system.

(b) The simulation to be repeated under precisely controlled conditions if, after examination of the initial results from the Analysis Program, further analysis and reclassification of the raw data is required.

7   ATC system modelling today

7.1 Although the use of modelling techniques in the analysis of ATC system problems is still at a very early stage, the techniques are gaining acceptance as potentially powerful research tools. It is therefore perhaps appropriate at this time briefly to attempt to examine what is being achieved and what may be expected in the future.

7.2 *Systems analysis.* The processes of ATC are as yet ill-defined, and in spite of a mass of regulations, largely depend upon many unwritten rules — experience. Consequently, any simulation task must essentially be undertaken by an integrated and experienced team of air traffic controllers, mathematicians, and programmers, capable of meaningful operational and logical analysis.

7.3 *Application.* As any results obtained can only be as good as the underlying systems analysis and basis of assumptions, successful modelling in ATC involves the expenditure of a good deal of expert effort, measurable in man years. Consequently, individual specific investigations are difficult to justify. Rather the aim should be to build a number of models at differing levels of complexity and scope, for continuing use over a period of time. Only in this way is it possible to accumulate the experience necessary to ensure that the models give an entirely adequate representation of the systems under study. GPS is currently engaged in four such projects building total system models both for immediate major investigations and for subsequent later use. Three of these models are in the nature of research tools and will be used in the development of long-term future system designs. The fourth model will be used in a substantial cost-effectiveness analysis and will be retained as an aid in the isolation of short-term system problems. It is envisaged that this model will be updated each year in the light of system changes and used with the air traffic input forecasts for the following year, in order to highlight the difficulties which may be expected to arise.

7.4 *Validation.* Perhaps one of the major myths in regard to A T C system modelling is that of absolute quantitative validation. Even in the most advanced of A T C systems the basic performance data with which to make such a validation is hard to find, and in general the task of mounting data-collection exercises is not practicable. Moreover, when using the techniques to gain an estimate of the response of the system to changed environmental conditions the *only* performance data available is derived from the simulation itself.

7.5 Under these circumstances it is possible only to make such comparisons as may be practicable in regard to system response characteristics and to attempt to evaluate the results on the basis of 'reasonableness'. Accordingly, therefore, simulation is as yet mainly employed to allow relative rather than absolute comparisons. However, experience gained during the past three years does indicate that it should be possible to obtain a good degree of correlation between actual and forecast system performance. In particular, for example, traffic delays at London Heathrow Airport are growing largely in accordance with forecasts derived from simulation some two years ago.

7.6 *Fast-time.* Hitherto, there has been a tendency to attempt to compare and quantify the efficiency of various A T C simulations on the basis of a 'fast-time coefficient', that is, the ratio of the period of real time simulated to the duration of computing time. But has this any real significance? As the traffic density is increased the number of activities per unit time becomes greater and, for a set interval of simulated time, the time required for computation gets progressively larger. Similarly, an increase in the complexity of the environment will, in general, lead to an increase in the computing time for each activity and a corresponding decrease in the 'fast-time coefficient', whilst the programming logic of the simulation remains unchanged. Since the coefficient is so dependent upon the input parameters, it cannot provide a suitable 'success' criterion to quantify a simulation, let alone a yard-stick, to compare models which may vary from the representation of a relatively small system composed of two terminal areas and their interconnecting airways to the representation of an environment extending over half of Europe. A more successful

I

criterion might be the 'fast-time coefficient' multiplied by the number of
ATC controllers, or work positions, envisaged for the actual system. This
has several obvious drawbacks, since the complexity of the logic will vary
from model to model, but may be useful in the absence of a better alternative criterion.

7.7 *Cost-effectiveness.* It will be seen that air traffic control simil-
ation is a complex and substantial task involving a large investment in
expert effort and computer time.

7.8 The limited experience available does not yet permit the derivation of any clear cost-effectiveness ratio. However, investigations to
date have led to the possibilities of establishing significant cost benefits
to airline operators through the reduction of air traffic control delays, and
modelling techniques are now facilitating air traffic control systems
analysis on a scale which would otherwise not be possible. A current task,
for example, involves the modelling of a large part of the upper European
airspaces under the jurisdiction of the Eurocontrol Agency, an area including many thousands of square miles and, at any one time, many hundreds
of aircraft carrying many thousand people.

7.9 The purpose of this model is to enable comparisons to be made,
at forecast traffic densities not yet experienced in Europe of alternative
route structures, ATC procedures, and varying degrees of dependence on
ground radar and airborne navigational capability. These comparisons will
be made in terms of penalties to operators and implications for ATC administration. The penalties will be assessed by such measures as route
mileage increases, delays and the flying of uneconomic profiles, whilst
the implications for ATC administration will be concerned with ATC
workload and the consequent requirements for staff and ground equipment.
Figures 2, 3 and 4 illustrate the GPS approach to the modelling of the
system.

7.10 It is hoped to isolate factors which are significant in the determination of system capacity and safety, to facilitate concentration of resources in those areas likely to be most fruitful, and above all to make a
contribution in the single socio-technological area which may be of the
greatest significance at this time — communications — the transport of
people and materials and the transfer of ideas.

7.11 *GPS simulation models.* The Appendix to this paper contains
details of ATC simulation models either completed or in hand at the
present time.

Fig. 1 UNITED KINGDOM CONTROLLED AIRSPACE

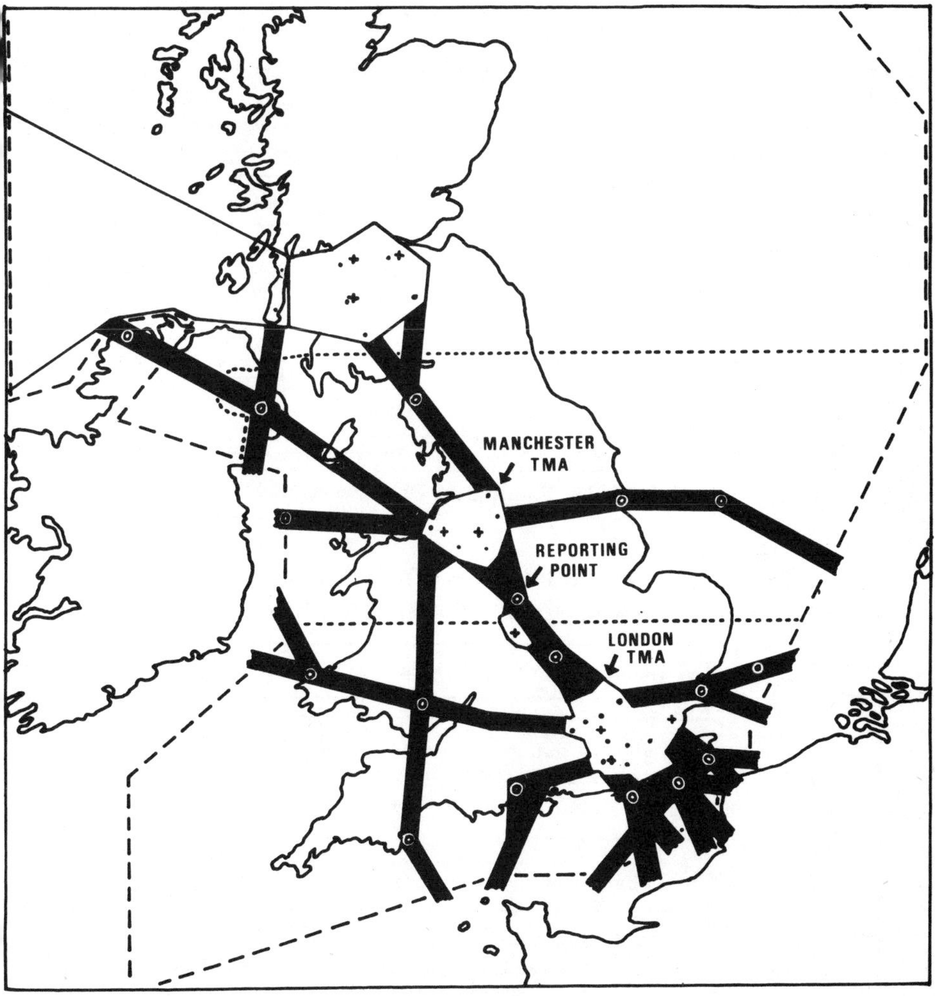

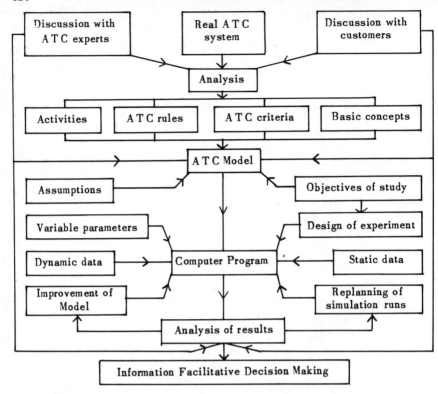

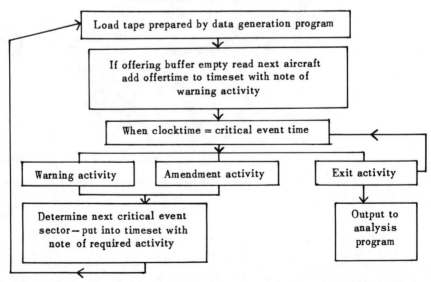

**SIMPLIFIED FLOW DIAGRAM FOR
EN-ROUTE SIMULATION PROGRAM**

Fig. 3 ACTIVITIES 125

For preferred track and level of first route choice

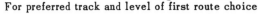

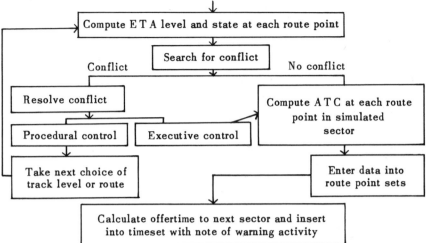

Compute E T A level and state at each route point

Search for conflict

Conflict | No conflict

Resolve conflict

Compute A T C at each route point in simulated sector

Procedural control | Executive control

Take next choice of track level or route

Enter data into route point sets

Calculate offertime to next sector and insert into timeset with note of warning activity

AMENDMENT ACTIVITY

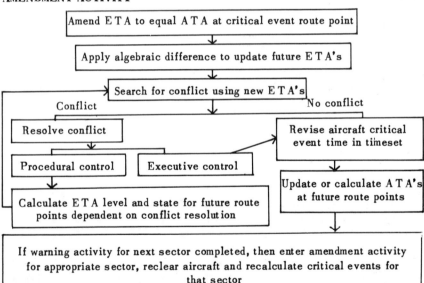

Amend E T A to equal A T A at critical event route point

Apply algebraic difference to update future E T A's

Search for conflict using new E T A's

Conflict | No conflict

Resolve conflict

Revise aircraft critical event time in timeset

Procedural control | Executive control

Update or calculate A T A's at future route points

Calculate E T A level and state for future route points dependent on conflict resolution

If warning activity for next sector completed, then enter amendment activity for appropriate sector, reclear aircraft and recalculate critical events for that sector

EXIT ACTIVITY

Output history of aircraft through sector, including conflict information. Determine actual executive control requirements and exposures to minimum separation

Delete aircraft from route point sets within sector and, if aircraft is leaving simulated area, delete from active aircraft SET

Fig. 4 EN-ROUTE MODEL

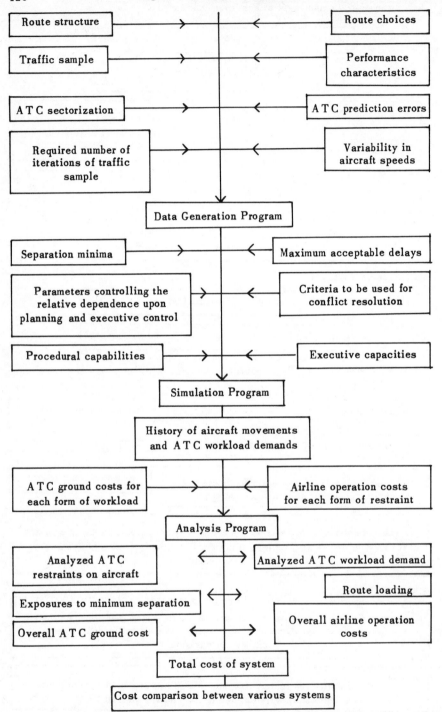

APPENDIX

SIMULATION CONTRACTS COMPLETED OR IN HAND

CLIENT	DESCRIPTION OF THE SIMULATION	STATUS
Decca Navigator Company	The development of a computer simulation model of outbound operations from the London Terminal Area. The object of the simulation was to establish the benefits, in reduction of delay and the use of non-optimum flight levels, if any, which would accrue to :- (a) a particular aircraft operator, and (b) to aircraft operators in general from the use of an area navigational capability by varying percentages of aircraft operating on Airway Amber 1 north of London.	COMPLETED
Decca Navigator Company	The development of an advanced Terminal Area and En-route Simulation Program which would permit evaluation and comparison of the probable system performance and operating costs of a particular ATC system given a specified navigational capability. The selected system comprised two complex Terminal Areas (representative of busy European TMAs) joined by a busy route. The evaluation was conducted using various route structure configurations (bi-directional routes and combinations of uni-directional parallel routes) and assuming the use of either point-source or area coverage navigational systems at the same traffic levels.	COMPLETED
The Eurocontrol Agency	This contract required the development of a 'general purpose' computer simulation program for the evaluation of all foreseeable combinations of techniques for the control of en-route traffic	

CLIENT	DESCRIPTION OF THE SIMULATION	STATUS
The Eurocontrol Agency	(including supersonic transport aircraft) within the entire Eurocontrol airspaces. These airspaces comprise the national Upper Airspaces of Belgium, France, Ireland, Luxemburg, Netherlands, West Germany and the United Kingdom. The model will be used in a Specific Investigation to prove the satisfactory operations of the model, to assess its capability and to examine the problems consequent upon the introduction of supersonic transport aircraft. The model will later be translated for subsequent use on the Eurocontrol T R 4 computer at Bretigny.	IN HAND
The Royal Radar Establishment	An air movement simulation model of a multi-airport Terminal Area will be developed to assess the contribution of improved radar data-gathering and processing systems in this environment and to assist in deducing the role and parameter of such systems. Development of this model has involved the design and evaluation of TMA route structure configurations using analytical and simulation methods and the model will enable quantitative assessment to be made of these route structures and the assumed radar capacity. It will also provide to the radar designer important data on the three-dimensional spacing of aircraft in the varying traffic situations occurring in the simulated environment.	IN HAND
The Government of Hong Kong	A computer simulation study for evaluation of the cost-effectiveness of several proposed modifications to the Hong Kong A T C system at various levels of traffic demand. The study has required the development of separate 'Runway' and 'Airspace' models, and, for selected system proposals, will provide quantitative measurements of system loading and performance which can be assessed in terms of staff and equipment requirements for agreed parameters of A T C delay and other A T C restriction to operators. The model will be general purpose in character and therefore capable of	IN HAND

CLIENT	DESCRIPTION OF THE SIMULATION	STATUS
The Government of Hong Kong	continuing use for the evaluation of any proposed system developments.	
The Eurocontrol Agency	The use of a fast-time simulation model to provide a quantitative assessment of the levels of air traffic at which route splitting would be required on European routes in the 1970's in order to maintain effective Air Traffic Control. The study is intended to contribute to the Agency's overall cost-effectiveness examination of the case for improved aircraft navigation.	IN HAND

MODELS OF FACT: EXAMPLES FROM MARKETING

A. S. C. EHRENBERG

'The basic question is: Take away the
mathematical language and what generalised
factual knowledge of the process in question
still remains? If the answer is none, the
mathematical symbol for that is very simple.'

CONTENTS

1   Sonking, or the Scientification of Non-Knowledge

What is a model supposed to model? There are two kinds of models, and
two kinds of model builders. On the one hand there is the scientist who
knows something and wants a model of what he knows.

On the other hand there is the man who does not know anything about
the system in question and wants to build a model of that. Reasons for
the popularity of this Scientification Of Non-Knowledge [1] are threefold:

Methodological: Sonking is entrenched in the O.R. approach
('First, young man, construct a model of the whole system').

Social: Sonking provides instant mathematics for decision-
makers in government and industry.

Psychological: Sonking allows the neo-cartesian modelling man to persuade himself of his own existence along well-trodden lines: 'I SONK, THEREFORE I AM'.

2   The statistical search for significance

On turning to models of fact, one finds however that factual discoveries tend nowadays to be dismissed as being deficient in theory:

'The result is *merely* empirical.'

The trouble is that the modern empiricists have given empiricism a bad name by reporting ISOLATED facts without any attempt at generalisation and integration, i.e. without in fact aiming to build up a comprehensive model !

'Sophisticated' scientists are still expected to end their papers with one-, two-, or three-star levels of significance for their experimental results, which is at best the *beginning* of analysis and not the end. As Gatty has recently put it [2]:

'Even discovering a significant correlation may not be very helpful without a great deal of further study. Statistical significance of a correlation coefficient, or of a regression coefficient, merely means that there is a pretty good chance that it is in fact a number different from zero. One should not exaggerate the worthwhileness of a coefficient simply because it probably differs from zero'.

3   Empirical generalisations, laws, and models

The drawback of an isolated finding is that it is isolated. What is needed is to establish under what empirical conditions it generalizes to form a 'law' [3]. Only then does it become worth trying to discover how different aspects of a system can be interrelated with each other, to form an empirically-based theory or model.

4   A practical example : the pattern of TV viewing

One practical example from marketing concerns the extent to which the same people watch television at different points in time. (Better understanding of viewing patterns is of potential value for programme-planning and sociological purposes as for example in studies for the Independent Television Authority, and in the efficient use of air-time for advertising as in work for J. Walter Thompson.)

Possible approaches to building a model of viewing patterns can be along the three lines indicated in Sections 1-3, as follows:

Firstly, one could begin by postulating a comprehensive stochastic model for the whole system:

'The audience at any time t is regarded as generated by sampling the ith individual from the population at risk with a probability which is related first to the audience size r_t at the time t and second to the ith individual's general intensity of viewing v_i ..... Ignoring ..., and assuming ..., the proportion d_{st} of the population who view at two times s and t will then be given by $d_{st} = ...,$ where ...'.

In the absence of any generalized knowledge of actual viewing patterns, this *a priori* approach would however do no more than model the model builder's probabilistic assumptions and empirical ignorance.

Secondly, the multivariate statistical approach would be to derive an equation between people's viewing patterns and a selection of all the kinds of complex factors which can influence them:

The time of day and day of the week for each viewing occasion, whether these occasions are on the same day or different days, the time of the year and the weather, the channel or station tuned to, the nature of the programmes that are being viewed, the programmes immediately preceding and following on that channel, the programmes on the opposing channels, feed-back effects of previous exposure to various types of programme, the audience levels at each point in time, the nature of the relevant population group, people's viewing and other needs as well as their attitudes and social habits, and so on and so on.

After making 'reasonable' assumptions about the form of the relationship between viewing behaviour and these explanatory variables, one would put a set of data through some multiple regression or component analysis or the like, and wait for significant coefficients to emerge.

Thirdly, the search for generalized lawlike relationships might start by looking for any simple pattern that may exist in some limited data, as for example the duplication of viewing data for Monday the 24th January and Thursday the 27th January, 1966, in London.

This is shown in Table 17 which is taken from a recent paper by W.A. Twyman [4]. The table gives the percentage of the population who viewed ITV (the 'rating') for the first ¼-hour in the hour from 5.00 p.m. to 11.00 p.m. on each of the two days, and also the 'duplicated' percentage of the population who viewed ITV both at some time s, say, on Monday, and at some time t on the Thursday.

It is not difficult to see that viewing at any time s on one day and viewing at any time t on the other day was correlated, and that these correlations can virtually all be accounted for by a single constant. Thus the duplicated audience d_{st} at times s and t on the two different days with ratings r_s and r_t can be described by the one-parameter relationship

$$d_{st} \doteqdot k r_s r_t,$$

TABLE 17

Duplication of viewing: Observed values and predicted values† of the percentage of housewives viewing at any two times on Monday and Thursday, January 24th and 27th, 1966 in London. ($K = 1 \cdot 3$)

Monday—¼-hour starting:	Rating	Thursday—¼-hour starting:						
		5 p.m. 8	6 p.m. 25	7 p.m. 43	8 p.m. 41	9 p.m. 34	10 p.m. 28	11 p.m. 18
5 p.m.	5	1 *1*	2 *2*	3 *3*	2 *3*	2 *2*	1 *2*	1 *1*
6 p.m.	24	5 *3*	14 *8*	14 *14*	12 *13*	10 *11*	10 *9*	6 *6*
7 p.m.	33	4 *3*	13 *11*	19 *19*	17 *18*	15 *15*	11 *12*	9 *8*
8 p.m.	43	4 *5*	14 *14*	23 *24*	22 *23*	19 *19*	16 *16*	9 *10*
9 p.m.	37	4 *4*	11 *12*	19 *21*	20 *20*	16 *17*	12 *14*	7 *9*
10 p.m.	28	2 *3*	8 *9*	15 *16*	14 *15*	14 *13*	10 *10*	8 *7*
11 p.m.	7	1 *1*	2 *2*	3 *4*	3 *3*	3 *3*	4 *3*	4 *2*

† Predicted values shown in italic figures.

where k is a constant — here $1 \cdot 3$ — for any two times s and t on the two days. The values $1 \cdot 3\, r_s r_t$ are shown in italics in Table 17 and fit the observed duplication values to within a mean deviation of ± 1 percentage points.

Nobody would be really interested in such a description of Londoners' duplicated viewing on a certain Monday and Thursday late in January 1966 if it were an isolated finding. But examination of several hundred other cases showed the relationship to hold under a wide range of empirical conditions, as summarised in Table I [4]. In addition, 3 000 recent cases Las Vegas and some 50 000 in the London and Northern TV Regions in Great Britain last year followed the same relationship, again within average limits of ± 1 [5].

This duplication result $d_{st} \doteqdot k\,r_s r_t$ is not a model of a complex system but a simple 'law' describing one aspect of a system. Something more like a fully-fledged 'model' begins to emerge when one can account for (or 'explain') the single parameter k in the law, for instance by relating it to some other aspect of viewing behaviour.

This kind of development was recently described by G.J. Goodhardt in *Nature* [6]. It follows the standard line of starting with an empirical generalization, positing an explanatory hypothesis, introducing an assumption, making a technical simplification to facilitate the analysis, skipping the mathematical details ('it is obvious that ...'), checking that the theoretical result agrees with the empirical facts, discovering that the basic finding (that k is a function of the viewing intensities) is a

TABLE I

Empirical conditions under which $d_{ts} = k r_t r_s \pm 1$ is known to hold
(d_{ts} is the duplicated audience at two times s and t on
two different days of the week with ratings r_s and r_t.)

Any two programmes	1959
Any two days of the week	1965
Any two ratings levels from 0 to about 50	1966
Any two times of day from 2 p.m. to 11.15 p.m.	
	Summer
Adults	Winter
HW's	
Sets on	London, ITV
	Great Britain, ITV
Continuous meter panels	Alabama, WRBC
Continuous diary panels	
1-week diary surveys	Two-channel
1-week recall surveys	Poly-channel*

* The phrase "poly-channel" has been devised by Mr N. L. Webb to distinguish multi-channel viewing situations with three or more operating channels from the two-channel situation which has been traditional in Great Britain until recently.

mathematical tautology anyway but all the more useful for that, and finally looking towards wider implications.

Because of its brevity, Goodhardt's note is reproduced in full. The contrast with the sonking approach outlined at the beginning of this section is that his theory [only] explains a well-established empirical generalisation.

Constant in Duplicated Television Viewing

CONSIDER the proportion of the audience viewing television at some time t who also view a given programme on the same television channel at a certain time s on another day of the week. It is then known that for all different times t this proportion remains approximately constant.

In its most general form this finding is best expressed by the empirical relationship $d_{st} = k r_s r_t \pm 0\cdot01$ between the proportion d_{st} of the total population who view the channel at both times s and t and the two audience levels or "ratings" r_s and r_t, where k is an empirical constant greater than 1. The part played by the content of a programme in attracting an audience therefore does not seem to act differentially across the population, but is summed up simply by the level of the audience which it attracts.

This simple empirical finding suggests a stochastic model in which the audience at any time s is regarded as generated by sampling the ith individual from the population at risk with a probability which is related first to the audience size r_s at time s and second to the individual's general intensity of viewing v_i. The latter quantity does not vary with the programme being shown and can be defined as the daily total hours viewed by the ith individual divided by the hours viewed by the average individual.

(Reprinted from Nature, Vol. 212, No. 5070, p. 1616 only, December 31, 1966)

Ignoring that in this model the "sampling" should be without replacement from a finite population, we have that the probability p_{is} of the ith individual viewing the sth segment of time is given as a first approximation by $p_{is} \doteq v_i r_s$. Assuming now that two times s and t on two different days are sufficiently far apart for the "sampling" to be independent, the proportion d_{st} of the population of n individuals who view at both times should be given by

$$d_{st} = \sum_i (p_{is}p_{it})/n = \{\sum_i (v_i' v_i'')/n\} r_s r_t$$

where v_i' and v_i'' are the ith individual's intensity of viewing on the two days. The summation term here is constant for all pairs of times s and t, and this theoretical relationship therefore agrees with the empirical result $d_{st} \doteq k r_s r_t$.

The constant k can be calculated either from the observed duplications d_{st}, as $k = \sum d_{st}/\sum(r_s r_t)$ where the summation is over all times s and t on 2 days, or from the daily intensities of viewing v_i', and v_i''. as $k = \sum(v_i' v_i'')/n$ where the summation is over all individuals i. It can be shown that these two expressions are mathematically identical.

Examination of English and American viewing data obtained by TAM, Research Services and ARB under a variety of conditions—for example, both recent and five or more years ago, for all transmission times on different days of the week, for adults in general as well as for housewives and for the popular "set-on" type of audience measure, and for four different audience measurement techniques—has shown that the values of k for any pair of days can vary from as little as $1\cdot2$ to as much as $2\cdot5$, but the relationship $d_{st} = k r_s r_t$ still holds within the average limits of fit of $\pm 0\cdot01$.

This possible explanation of the empirical duplication of viewing law in terms of the general intensity of people of viewing now provides a basis for examining the patterns of television viewing in general, and the wider implications of this finding are being investigated.

G. J. GOODHARDT

5   A second example : the pattern of consumer purchasing

The study of consumer purchasing behaviour for non-durable branded household goods and the like provides a second case-history where a much wider range of empirical generalizations have however already been subsumed in a single theory or model. (Consumer purchasing behaviour is of course central to marketing, and better understanding of it, as in work for Esso Petroleum, ICI Fibres, J. Walter Thompson and Unilever, can lead to a variety of practical applications [e.g. 7, 8, 9]).

The three approaches to model building which were distinguished earlier can again be identified.

Firstly, there is already quite a history of speculative model building. For example, repeated attempts have been made to apply first-order homogeneous stationary Markov theory to repeat-buying and brand-switching concepts, references being given in an earlier paper [10]. But this appears to have been done without much recourse to real data. Two possible reasons are that measurements of consumer purchasing behaviour are generally of the wrong form to feed into a Markov system, and that the assumptions of Markov theory do not apply to the empirical situation.

Secondly, the statistical approach of explaining things by multiple regression or the like has led to many isolated coefficients being reported. Some typical examples were recently given by Frank, Green and Siebert [11], who in effect report findings like 'the multiple adjusted R^2 between average price paid for Regular Coffee and 22 selected socio-economic and purchasing-behaviour variables was ·48, in our data'. And so on.

Thirdly, the empirical 'look-and-see' approach of searching for simple regular patterns in some quite narrow area has led to a variety of empirical generalizations during the last ten years or so. These relate to repeat-buying behaviour for any given brand or pack-size in successive time-periods when there is no overall trend in its sales.*

A few of these empirical regularities are illustrated in Table 3 which is taken from a current report [9] and shown on page 141 at the end of this paper. Three examples are:

(a) That the percentage of total sales of a brand in a given period which is accounted for by so-called repeat-buyers (people who also bought in the preceding time-period) is monotonically related to the average number of units w bought per buyer.

(b) That this percentage of sales accounted for by repeat-buyers is approximately the same as the percentage of sales accounted for by the buyers of more than one unit in the time-period. (Compare the two **bold** columns in Table 3).

(c) That the average number of units bought per 'new' buyer (buyers who did *not* buy the brand in the previous time-period) is roughly constant, at about 1·4 or so.

Many other such empirical regularities in repeat-buying behaviour have been discussed and documented elsewhere [e.g. 12 and 13].

Table 3 (page 141) also shows how these kinds of findings hold under a wide range of different empirical conditions. For instance, reading the table from left to right, they hold for a wide variety of product-fields,

---

* It is as well to understand this kind of 'stationary' situation if one wants for example either to produce a change in it (e.g. an increase in sales) or to evaluate what one has achieved by comparing the results with what would have happened in the absence of change (again the stationary situation).

TABLE III

Empirical conditions under which various aspects of the stationary purchasing model are known to hold

> Percentage of buyers ranging from almost 0% to 50% or more
> The 4 to 6 leading brands in each product-field
> Large, medium and small pack-sizes
> Great Britain
> Continental Europe
> U.S.A.
> From 1950 to 1966
> Summer/Winter
> Different demographic sub-groups (size of household, etc.)
> Buying behaviour in periods of 1 week to 6 months or more
> Different product-fields including bread, breakfast cereals, butter, canned vegetables, cat and dog foods, clothing, cocoa, coffee, confectionery, cooking fats, detergents, disinfectants, fruit drinks, household soaps, household cleaners, jams and marmalade, margarine, petrol, polishes, processed cheese, sausages, shampoos, soft drinks, soup, toilet paper, toilet soap

different brands in the same product-field, different times and different places, and (further over to the right) different market penetration (% buying), different sales levels, different lengths of time-period, varying buying patterns for other brands in the same product-field, and differing marketing activities more generally. In all, a few thousand cases have been covered so far, the degree of empirical generalization being summarised in Table III [3].

Each of the relationships illustrated in Table 3 (page 141) represents a separate empirical generalization. To build an integrated 'model' for these various laws, each law must first be expressed in a convenient form, i.e. as a mathematical equation. Different mathematical functions can be used to within some reasonable degree of approximation. What particular type of function is initially used does not greatly matter, because it is quite likely to be adjusted in subsequent work [see 14].

In describing the apparent relationships in Table 3 it is convenient (as discussed further below) to reformulate w, the average number of units bought per buyer, as a certain parameter q defined by the implicit relationship

$$w = - q / (1 - q) \ln (1 - q).$$

The observed percentage of sales which is accounted for by repeat-buyers (the first **bold** column of figures in Table 3) is then approximately equal to

$$q.$$

An alternative representation in the most usual parameter-space $2 < w < 20$ is as an explicit function of w,

$$1.23 \, (w - 1)^{1.23} / \{ 1.23 \, (w - 1)^{1.23} + \tfrac{1}{2} \}$$

Both these equations hold for the data in Table 3 (and also more generally) to within average limits of about ± 3 percentage points.*

Next, the percentage of sales accounted for by buyers of at least 2 units — as shown by the second **bold** column for the 20 cases in Table 3 for example — is similarly represented by the above 1, 2, 3 expression in w. The neater formulation in terms of q, viz.

$$q,$$

has the advantage of being a special case of a more general descriptor

$$q^{r-1}$$

for the percentage of sales accounted for the buyers of at least r units, for any value of r greater or equal to 1.** In the case of the Table 3 data for example, this holds to within about ± 3 percentage points on average (except when the special 'shelving' or 'variance discrepancy' pattern operates — see [12]).

Other empirical laws of stationary puchasing behaviour are a little more complex in their q-formulation, but some simplify on approximating in the mnemonic 1, 2, 3-type of language used above. For example, the proportion of repeat-buyers from one period to the next is given by

$$1 + \ln(1 + q) / \ln(1 - q)$$
$$\doteqdot 2(1 - w) / (1 - 2.3w), \text{ for } 2 < w < 20.$$

Again, the average number of units bought per repeat-buyer in each period is

$$- q^2 / (1 - q) \ln(1 - q^2),$$
$$\doteqdot 1.23w, \text{ for } w > 1.5.$$

The latter relationship simply says that under stationary conditions, the repeat-buyers' average rate of buying is about 20% higher than that of all buyers. This relationship holds empirically to within a mean deviation of about .1 or .2 units for the various brands and product-fields and lengths of time-period which have been studied [e.g. 12, 13].

An even simpler finding is that the average number of units bought

---

* The numerical values of $100q$ corresponding to the 20 observed w's in Table 3 are 40, 47, 66, 69, 66, 76, 80, 81, 84, 86, 87, 87, 90, 90, 90, 92, 92, 93, 95 and 97. (Note the need to multiply by 100 to convert proportions to percentages).

** Since the expression q^{w-1} is approximately constant at .75, buyers of more than the average amount w of any stationary brand in any time-period account for roughly three-quarters of its total sales (as may for example be seen for the data in Table 3, interpolating for $r = w$).

per 'new' buyer is given by

$$q/\ln(1+q),$$
$$\doteqdot 1{\cdot}4 \text{ for } w > 2, \text{ i.e. a constant.}$$

The observed values recorded in Table 3 tend to be a little high, the mean deviation from 1·4 being ·2.

The form of the above equations makes it obvious that they did not spring to life by any kind of 'empirical curve-fitting'. Instead, they are all derived from the so-called LSD or Logarithmic Series Distribution model of stationary purchasing behaviour. The importance of this model is that it has both subsumed and integrated various *separate* empirical generalizations which had been established previously, often in quite a different mathematical form [see 12].

The one-parameter LSD model itself follows from an earlier and more general multivariate two-parameter NBD or Negative Binomial Distribution formulation as an approximation which can be summarized for $i = 1 - t$ stationary time-periods of lengths T_i by the probability generating function

$$\left\{ 1 + a \sum_{i=1}^{t} T_i(1 - u_i) \right\}^{-k},$$

where $a = q/(1 - q)$, the u_i are dummy variables, and k is very small.

6   Validity, meaning and practical usefulness

One reason for having discussed the two marketing models in Sections 4 and 5 is that they not only account for the illustrative data in Tables 3 and 17, but that some £100 000 000 worth of further data covering television viewing and consumer purchasing behaviour exists in Western Europe and the U.S.A. This acts as a check on the descriptive validity and practical usefulness of the models.

As regards their *meaning*, the modern treatment of model building as a new art seems to seek for 'real' meaning in some underlying stochastic formulation. Such a formulation happens to exist for both the models here, namely Goodhardt's simulated sampling scheme by which television programmes pick their viewers [6], and a compound Poisson formulation from which the NBD/LSD model of repeat-buying behaviour can be derived [see 12].

Such probabilistic gymnastics can be stimulating and of immense technical value to the model builder himself. However, it does not seem to add either to the basic validity or to the practical usefulness of a descriptive model of fact.

TABLE 3

The Percentage of Total Sales Accounted for by Repeat-Buyers and by Buyers of at least r units, and other Observed Statistics

Approximately stationary brands over two equal time-periods: Twenty varied case-histories

| | | | | | % OF SALES ACCOUNTED FOR | | | | | | | | | | | | | |
| | | | BASIC | PROPORTIONAL TO w | | | | | | | | | CONSTANT | NOT DIRECTLY RELATED TO w | | | | |
PRODUCT	BRAND	Time & Place	Av. Units bght. per buyer: w	by Repeat-Buyers	by Buyers of at least r units, for r = 2	3	4	6	8	12	16	20	Av. Units bght. per "new" buyer	Buyers %	Sales: Units per 100 Inf.	Period in Weeks	Buying of Other Brands	Marketing Activities
Soap Flakes	A	Midl. '65	1.3	45	41	21	8	3					1.2	2***	3	12		
Clothing	B	U.K. '66	1.4	55	54	17	8						1.5	45	63	1		
Flour	C	U.S. '51	1.8	65	67	41	41	13					1.6	21***	36	13		
Soap Flakes	A	Midl. '65	1.9	*	67	53	29	16					*	4***	8	24		
Detergent	D	Lancs.'63	1.8	69	72	39	25						1.3	8***	14	4		
Detergent	E	Lancs.'63	2.2	83	81	59	40	[6]					1.3	21	45	4	U	U
Soap Flakes	F	Midl. '65	2.5	82	78	70	58	38					1.3	4***	10	12	N	N
Drink	G	U.K. '55	2.6	76	81	68	55	39	29	19			1.6	15	38	13	S	S
Detergent	H	Lancs.'63	2.9	84	88	80	54	[27]	[27]**				1.6	14	40	4	P	P
Fuel	I	U.K. '66	3.1	85	89	78	63	[36]	[21]	[6]	[4]**		1.8	27	85	4	B	B
Drink	G	U.K. '53	3.3	*	87	76	65	49	37	22	14	11	*	19	63	26	C	C
Detergent	D	Lancs.'63	3.3	78	88	74	67	48	38	[18]	[3]**		1.7	13	43	12	I	I
Soap Flakes	F	Midl. '65	3.8	*	88	82	74	56	46	32	17		*	5	19	24	F	F
Soap Flakes	J	U.S. '51	3.9	89	90	82	67	62	46	33			1.5	16***	65	13	I	I
Margarine	K	U.S. '51	3.9	87	91	84	72	72	53	33	33	15	1.8	26***	100	13	B	B
Soup	L	U.K. '58	4.7	*	94	87	82	71	63	50	38	30	*	14	66	26	D	D
Detergent	D	Lancs.'63	4.7	93	94	89	84	67	55	[20]	[3]**		1.6	30	140	12		
Fuel	I	U.K. '66	4.8	*	94	88	84	69	58	[32]	[15]	[8]	*	46	221	8		
Detergent	H	Lancs.'63	6.2	94	96	93	90	86	75	47	[26]	[26]	1.7	18	108	12		
Detergent	H	Lancs.'63	10.1	*	98	95	93	91	87	77	64	[49]	*	22	219	24		

*Repeat-buying information not available.

**"Shelving" pattern – see reference 3.

***Less than 50 buyers in sample

References

[1] 'America and the Rest — Some Comparisons'. (1967). *Commentary*, **9**, 12-21.

[2] 'Multivariate Analysis for Marketing Research'. (1966). *Applied Statistics*, **15**, 157-172.

[3] 'Laws in Marketing', (1966). *Applied Statistics*, **15**, 257-267.

[4] 'On Measuring Television Audiences', (1967). *J. Roy. Statist. Soc. A.*, **130**, 1-59.

[5] 'A Necessary Step in Television Research'. Read at the Annual Conference of the AMA, Toronto, June 1967.

[6] 'The Constant in Duplicated Television Viewing'. (1966). *Nature*, **212**, 5070, 1616.

[7] 'Ten Questions about Consumer Purchasing and Some Answers'. (1966). *Advertising Quarterly*, **9**, 3-8.

[8] 'Conditional Trend Analysis: A Breakdown by Initial Purchasing Level'. (1967). *J. Marketing Research*, **4**, 155-161.

[9] 'The Practical Meaning and Usefulness of the NBD/LSD Theory of Repeat-Buying'. To be read at the Research and Ind. Appl. Section Conference of the R.S.S., Brighton, September, 1967.

[10] 'An Appraisal of Markov Brand-Switching Models'. (1965). *J. Marketing Research*, **2**, 347-362.

[11] 'Household Correlates of Purchase Price for Grovery Products'. (1967). *J. Marketing Research*, **4**, 54-58.

[12] 'Progress on a Simplified Model of Stationary Consumer Purchasing Behaviour'. (1966). *J. Roy. Statist. Soc. A.*, **129**, 317-367.

[13] 'A Comparison of American and British Repeat-Buying Habits'. (1967). Aske Research Inc.

[14] 'The Elements of Lawlike Relationsips'. (1966). A report prepared for Unilever. Aske Research Ltd.,

MODEL BUILDING AND SCIENTIFIC METHOD
A GRAPHIC INTRODUCTION

H. O. WOLD

As my talk comes towards the end of this conference, I have an opportunity to place what I want to say in perspective, against the background of the wide-ranging discussion about model building covered by previous speakers. I shall also make one or two comments on what they have said. What I have to say is mainly expository.[1] But perhaps I may draw attention to two points on which my remarks may cover new ground. The first of these is the distinction between models of low information content and those of high information content; the second concerns the irreversibility (or, in other words, the asymmetrical nature) of the relationship between variables which enter into the kind of models we are discussing. I shall return to these points later.

Model building of the kind we have discussed at this conference is at the crossroads between two different lines of development. The first is the transition from deterministic to probabilistic models; the second is the transition from uni-relational to multi-relational models. This double transition has created several difficulties, and I will comment on three of them. These particular difficulties have all been important stumbling blocks; each in its time has been a topic of the day. The first is known as the choice of regression and was much debated before the Second World War. The second, which concerns the nature and solution of systems of simultaneous equations, has been much debated since the war. And the third, which is just coming into the picture, is the problem of reversibility.

It so happens that these three stumbling blocks are of a rather technical nature. This means that when you want to build a model in which these problems occur, you cannot avoid them. You have to answer them one way or the other. In other words it is essential for practical purposes that the model builder takes some sort of attitude towards them. At the same time these technical questions are closely related to fundamental questions about the principles of scientific method. This means that, in order to discuss them, you have somehow to cover a wide range of argument, extending right from the fundamental level to the technical level.

---

[1] Much of the material is borrowed from four recent papers, Ref. 22-25.
Also cf. Ref. 16.

This is rather difficult in forty-five minutes, but I will try to do it — by referring you to earlier papers about the detailed technical arguments, and with the help of a number of charts.

First, then, one or two comments of a basic nature. Model building, I think most people agree, is nothing other than scientific method. Scientific method is model building. To put it in the words of Enders A. Robinson, the actual output of research is a flow of models.[1] These

Chart 1 Retrospective inference v. forecasting. From Ref. 22.

models are either new models or developed versions of earlier models. Sometimes they overlap one another, sometimes they conflict with one another, and so on ; there is no end of the variety of models. When we look at models in this way we are taking a pluralistic view of science. Science is not unified; we think of it as a plurality, an enormous plurality of models. Conceptually, each model is to be regarded as a frame of reference, containing an empirical content and a theoretical content which have to be matched together in some way or other. I see model building as a process of matching an adequate theory to the empirical evidence.

My next point is a semantic one, which tends to cause confusion. It concerns the words 'description' and 'explanation'. Some philosophers use the word 'description' to refer to any statement about phenomena in the world around us ; anything you say, according to this usage, is description. Another usage distinguishes between description and explanation. We can illustrate this by considering the relationship between fertilizer on the one hand and the yield of a crop — wheat — on the other. As we give more fertilizer, the yield rises. This is a causal relationship: changes in the yield are explained by changes in the amount of fertilizer. Thus, according to the second usage we call this an explanation, while

---

[1] Incorporated in a Symposium summary, Ref. 20.

according to the first usage it is just a piece of description. This difference of usage has been a source of endless confusion. I want to make it clear that, in what I have to say, I adopt the second usage and make a distinction between description and explanation.

My next point is that, since model building is equivalent to scientific method, there are a number of important distinctions and classifications to be made between different kinds of models. At this conference several of these distinctions have been made by previous speakers: experimental models and non-experimental models; descriptive models and explanatory models; and so on. I want to point out one other type of distinction, the distinction between models with a low information content and those with a high information content. With some models, we have very little information to put in — whether as a basis for constructing the model or as input to it. At the other extreme we have a high level of information input. Both types of model are important and relevant, but my talk is mainly concerned with high information models, and I want to say only a word or two about low information models.

An example of low information models is, of course, to be found in stochastic models, where the stochastic element involves uncertainty. But we have to distinguish between two types of uncertainty in models of this kind. In one case, the uncertainty may be regarded as neutral so far as the model builder is concerned. To simplify, one may say that the model builder gets things more or less right if he hits upon the average value of the uncertain variable or variables. That is a reasonably favourable situation. But the second case is much less favourable and more difficult to deal with. For this is the case where the uncertainty is not just neutral, but positively antagonistic. We are here talking about situations of conflict — competitive business and military situations are typical cases in point — situations where the uncertainty is deliberately created and exploited by the enemy. The model in question thus has to be a low information model, you have to fight the enemy although you do not know what he is up to. Models of competitive situations of this kind form a very broad and important field of study. Group simulation by way of war games, business games, etc. is a widely used approach to construct and develop such models. Group simulation however has only recently come to the fore and is full of difficulties, which explains why so little has yet been achieved. It is not a sign of pessimism or a criticism of what has been done in this field, to say that the subject is still in its infancy and full of unresolved difficulties.

However, the three problems or stumbling blocks to which I referred and which are the main topic of my talk relate to high information models and not to low information models. They arise in the situation where we have experience of a kind which can be formulated as hypotheses in terms of functional relations with numerical parameters and where, therefore, we have a fairly good grip on the theoretical structure of the model. At the same time difficulties arise from the transition from deterministic to stochastic models and from uni-relational models which I have mentioned. I now propose to concentrate on these three topics and not to discuss further the problems of low information models or, in particular, the situation of antagonistic uncertainty.

It is important to distinguish between retrospective models and predictive models. This distinction is illustrated in Chart 1, where I use the Roman god Janus as a symbol. With one face Janus looks back into the past to discover regularities; with the other he looks forward into the future and attempts to make forecasts on the basis of the regularities he has discovered in the past. In order to do this he has to satisfy himself that the regularities which he has observed in the past will also hold for the future. This is what everybody actually does — there is nothing new in what I am saying. But perhaps for someone who has not thought very much about forecasting before, this is an easy way of understanding what it is about.

The important thing, then, is to establish what kind of regularities we have in the past. In particular, we have to distinguish between experimental regularities and non-experimental regularities. Experimental regularities are reproducible, because experiments are reproducible at any time and any place — that is the point of experiments. So if Janus can look at the results of experiments that have been made in the past, similar experiments can be made again in the future, and he is in a very favourable position; the question of how far past regularities will hold in the future need not cause trouble.

One or two examples may be helpful here. The first one, shown in Chart 2 which is taken from one of the statistical text books, demonstrates the regularity which emerges as one tosses a coin. If the coin is tossed up to four hundred times and the frequency with which heads and tails occur is measured after two throws, five throws, ten, twenty, fifty and so on up to four hundred, you find that the frequency tends toward an equal number of heads and tails. This is a descriptive experiment, inasmuch as we are interested in *what* happens in each throw — heads or tails — and not *why* a specific throw gives, say, heads. Other experiments might be explanatory, in the sense that they explain one variable in terms of another: in such and such a situation we get such and such response. Chart 3, taken from the book by Heady and Dillon, shows the results of rather a sophisticated experiment, in which total corn yield is related to varying quantities of phosphate fertilizer and three different levels of nitrate. These results are reproducible, and hold for similar soils and similar climates.

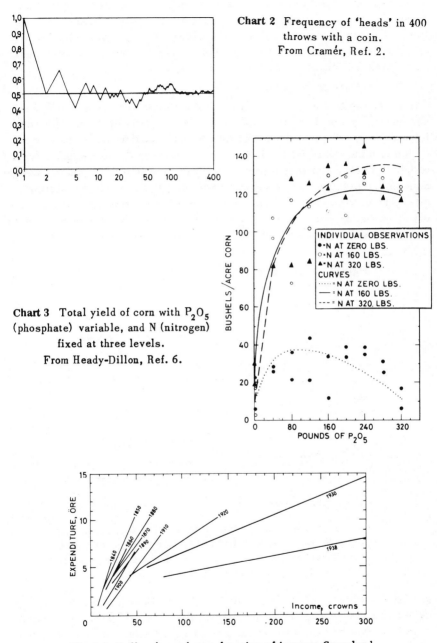

Chart 2 Frequency of 'heads' in 400 throws with a coin. From Cramér, Ref. 2.

Chart 3 Total yield of corn with P_2O_5 (phosphate) variable, and N (nitrogen) fixed at three levels. From Heady-Dillon, Ref. 6.

Chart 4 Coffee demand as a function of income; Greenland 1840-1938 (after P.P. Sveistrup). Individual budget data; 1 crown = 100 öre. From Ref. 26.

Forecasting problems occur, then, mainly in non-experimental situations. Non-experimental forecasting in most situations is essentially difficult. The future will not necessarily follow the same pattern as the past, and it is therefore of crucial importance to select those regularities in the past which will enable us to forecast the future.

Here are one or two examples.

Chart 4 shows household data for the Eskimos analysed over a period of one hundred years. It demonstrates that the elasticity of demand for coffee is practically zero over the whole time from the beginning. In other words, coffee is a necessity for the Eskimos. It is curious that these primitive people from the polar region provide us with the earliest example of household data. This does not mean, of course, that the Eskimos are statistically minded. It so happened that there was a Danish monopoly which traded with them which was statistically minded. This enterprise kept records for each family of Eskimos from 1840 onwards, and these records have been analysed.

Chart 5 gives another example.

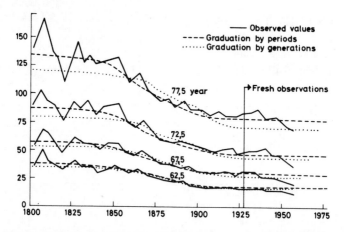

Chart 5 Mortality in Sweden 1800-1965, females, high age groups: thick lines. Mortality graduated 1800-1930 and forecast 1931-1960 by two methods (from Ref. 3): graduation by calendar years (broken curves); graduation by cohorts (dotted curves).

It refers to a study which Professor Cramér and I did in the early 1930s, on mortality in Sweden. The graph shows the results of forecasting future mortality rates by two different methods, on the basis of past trends, from 1931 onwards, and shows how these forecasts now compare with actual observations. It shows that in the mid-1940s there is a break in the trend, and this illustrates an important point. Some kind of innovation has taken place, which leads to great difficulty for Janus; for if there is an innovation, a real break with the past, there is no possibility of using the past to forecast the future. We have to find some way of studying the innovation itself and identifying its character. What happened in this case was that antibiotics were developed in the Second World War and led to sharply reduced mortality rates, thus making it no longer possible to forecast future mortality on the basis of the past.

The se two examples show that forecasting in non-experimental situations can be of a widely differing degree of difficulty. At the one extreme, of which the Eskimos' consumption of coffee is an example, we have relatively simple situations; at the other extreme we have situations which are so difficult we can do nothing about them. Here is an example of a difficult case (Chart 6).

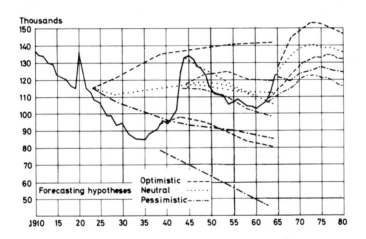

Chart 6 Annual births in Sweden 1900-1919 : thick black curve. Coloured curves (here reproduced by broken, dotted or stippled curves) : various forecasts. Cf. Ref. 16.

It concerns birth-rate forecasts in Sweden, and everyone knows how difficult it is to forecast the birth-rate. The solid curve shows actual births and the various dotted curves show the different forecasts which have been made. The solid curve seems very mysterious, as if it was doing its best to avoid the forecasts. In the mid-1930s the reproduction rate had fallen to 0·85 and people were afraid that in one generation we might lose 25 per cent of the Swedish population — then there were optimistic forecasts, pessimistic forecasts, neutral forecasts ; and the actual course of events was different from every prediction. The most drastic thing that happened is shown at the end of the graph, where the actual course of events very soon turned out entirely different from the original forecasts, and completely new forecasts had to be made. But in spite of examples like this, it is sometimes very difficult to persuade people that forecasts are not easy to make.

Time series analysis places at our disposal a variety of specialized techniques of forecasting. Chart 7 illustrates a key distinction, viz. between situations allowing unlimited versus limited predictability. The first is illustrated here by tidal water, the motion of which is known to be generated by the moon. Tidal waves can be forecast with very great accuracy over almost any length of time and the forecast is therefore unlimited.

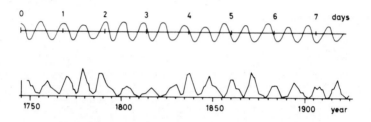

Chart 7 The lunar periodicity of tidal water (upper curve). The 11 year cycle in sunspot frequency (lower curve). From Ref. 24.

The second type of situation is illustrated by sunspot frequency. On Chart 7 the sunspots are plotted from 1750 up to 1925. The data were analysed by Yule in his famous paper of 1927. Here the periods of the fluctuations are irregular. If we try to apply Fourier analysis it does not work. Yule then introduced his classic model of the pendulum disturbed by a system of random shocks to represent fluctuations of the sunspot type. Yule's model allows forecast over a short time span, but as the range is extended the forecast becomes less informative and in the limit reduces to the overall average over time. This idea is, of course, now famous. Incidentally, I should like to comment at this point on the remark that the development of stochastic processes has been relatively slow in England. One reason I think is that up to the First World War science was somewhat national in character whereas it became much more international after the First World War, partly thanks to the scientific agencies of the League of Nations. It seems to me that England was rather slow in taking up this international attitude of research. Yule's model (1927) was brought to full significance in the international development in the theory and application of stochastic processes in the 1930s, and it was a forceful stimulus in the ensuing English developments.

I now turn to some simpler cases to illustrate the three stumbling blocks which I mentioned earlier. The first, you remember, was choice of regression. Chart 8 shows time series data in the field of market statistics, and is based on a Swedish study.

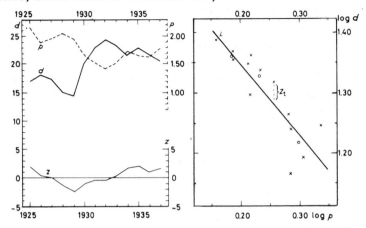

Chart 8 Market statistics for butter; co-operative stores in Stockholm, 1925-37. From Ref. 26.

a Data plotted as time series.   *b* Data plotted as a scatter diagram.
Ordinary scales.   Logarithmic scales.

It shows the price of butter in the Co-operative Stores in Stockholm from 1925 to 1937, and the demand for butter per member of these Co-operative Societies. If we plot in a scatter diagram we get thirteen points; the regression of demand on price gives us one line and the regression of price on demand gives us another. Of course, that was known from the beginning of regression theory, about 1900. The problem arose for the first time in econometrics, I think, when the Danish economist Mackeprang in 1906 studied the demand for coffee in these terms. He calculated both regressions and got rather different results — indeed one was some 25 per cent higher than the other. So he threw up his hands and said : 'Which of them shall we use? I do not know ! Here is a problem.'

This problem was much debated in the 1920s and '30s. The standard reference is Schultz's book 'The Theory and Measurement of Demand'. He carries through scores of regression analyses, each time calculating the two regressions of demand on price and price on demand, but he has no general principle about which regression to choose. This was the picture when I was asked by a government committee in Sweden to analyse some Swedish data. The regression problem was then such a topical one — you had to face it and reach a decision about it one way or the other. To cut a long story short, I pointed out the similarity between the relationship between price and demand and that between stimulus and response, price being the stimulus to which the consumer reacts by way of response. In the stimulus/response case there is no problem ; you always take the regression of response on stimulus. I argued that this is what one should do in the price/demand case as well.

Considerably later, around 1960, I developed this argument in terms of conditional expectations ; Refs. 17, 18. We assume that y is a function of x (a hypothetical function plus a residual error) and then we assume that this function gives the conditional expectation of y for a given value of x. In the simplest case, where we make the hypothetical function linear, the model is

$$\begin{cases} y = \alpha + \beta x + \epsilon \\ E(y \mid x) = \alpha + \beta x \end{cases} \tag{1}$$

and the problem is to estimate the unknown constants α and β. For the corresponding least squares regression of y upon x we write

$$y = a + bx + e \tag{2}$$

The constant β and its estimate b are of special relevance for the operative use of model (1) in applied work: if x changes by the amount Δ, the corresponding expected change in y is $\beta \Delta$; in improvised symbols,

$$E(y \mid x \to x + \Delta) \to y + \beta \Delta \tag{3}$$

The notions (1) – (2) and the inference (3) allow straightforward extension to multiple regression of y upon several variables $x_1, \ldots, x_h$.

In experimental data, where the x's are fixed, it was well known that under customary assumptions about the residuals the least squares estimates are maximum likelihood and unbiased.[1] in non-experimental data, where x's are not at choice the problem was open. There was even a lot of confusion about the problem. An interesting reference is a paper by Hurwicz in the monograph of 1950 by the Cowles commission, where he considers a linear regression defined by a conditional expectation ; he explores the small sample bias of least squares regression, and comments that he has tried, without success, to show that the regression is inconsistent; that is, biased in the large-sample sense. I cannot say I was influenced by his paper; it was only later on that it occurred to me that he had stated the problem so clearly there, and had made a wrong conjecture. It is very easy to see, in fact, that if you assume the hypothetical function is a conditional expectation, then it follows as a theorem that the least squares estimators are consistent. So there is no longer any question of being able to prove an inconsistency. The only curious thing is why the

---

1 For a many-faceted review, see Ref. 8.

author did not take the matter a bit further, and try to prove consistency
instead. His paper occurs in a volume devoted to multi-relational models,
for which least squares methods are known to yield large-sample bias,
and he was probably influenced by this fact to try to prove the same property for uni-relational models.

Coming to the second stumbling block, simultaneous equations, a key
feature is the distinction between causal chains versus interdependent
systems. Causal chains were introduced by Tinbergen in the 1930s and
for illustration he used arrow schemes of the type shown in chart 9 below.

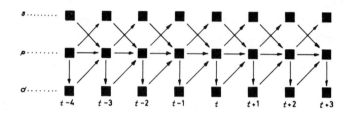

Chart 9 Arrow scheme for a causal chain system with three relations.
From Ref. 26.

Tinbergen's models were more complicated than this because his
systems were large, some 20 relations or more. The present example is
a simple case with three relations concerning supply, demand and price.

Such diagrams illustrate what one may think of as a flow of causation.
In simple cases (known as vector regression) we may regard what happens
in one period as influencing the following period, or equivalently, each
variable is dependent on the past but not on the other variables at the
same point of time. The models are then in the nature of lagged regression
combined with autoregression. Such models often arise in the physical
sciences because variables are regarded as continuous and their motion
expressed by differential equations. In econometrics continuous records
are not available and a good deal happens between the points of observation. Thus the problem of causal chains versus interdependent systems
is a new type of problem.

The causal chain type of model sets up a system under which the
current variables have a causal order. The first variable is influenced
only by the past, the second variable is influenced by the past but can
also be influenced by the current value of the first variable, the third is
influenced by the past and also possibly by the current values of the
second and first and so on.

This was the type of model which Tinbergen introduced in an intuitive
way. Somewhat later the spotlight of econometric research turned to a more

L

general type of model called interdependent systems, introduced in 1943
by the Norwegian economist Haavelmo. In contrast to causal chains, interdependent systems do not impose a causal order among the current
observations; they are assumed to be interdependent. In the equations of
a causal chain arranged in order the matrix of coefficients on the right
has zeros in the main diagonal and above the main diagonal. In an interdependent system there is no such distinction. The coefficients must be
zero in the main diagonal but otherwise they can be non-zero above or
below. It will be noted that Tinbergen's causal chain systems can be seen
as a generalization of Yule's model from uni-relational to multi-relational
approaches.

According to a key proposition in Haavelmo's paper, least squares
regression is inconsistent if applied to multi-relational models. This was
very much to my concern because I had used least squares for the estimation of uni-relational models in earlier studies, and Haavelmo's sweeping
proposition threw some doubt on such work inasmuch as any uni-relational
model can be conceived of as part of a multi-relational model. Hence I had
to reconsider the matter. An early result from 1946, due to Professor
Bentzel and myself, Ref. 1, specified causal chains and interdependent
systems as two distinct types of models, and it was shown that least
squares regression as applied to causal chains under general conditions
is equivalent to maximum likelihood estimation, and thereby consistent,
whereas it will in general be inconsistent if applied to interdependent
systems.

This last result raises new questions about interdependent systems.
The problems are difficult and there are many others still to explore but
I think that one important clue is the interpretation in terms of conditional
expectations. Since least squares regression is inconsistent if applied to
interdependent systems, it follows as a logical conclusion that such
systems do not constitute conditional expectations, and hence that they
do not provide a basis for inference of type (3). But if the relationships
are not conditional expectations what are they, and what is their operative
use, if any? I keep emphasizing this problem, and I am afraid that in some
econometric circles I am regarded in the light of Dennis the Menace, because I insist on its importance. Well, a constructive answer can be
obtained at the price of a slight re-specification of the model. The situation is very much related to H. Theil's method of two-stage least squares,
Ref. 12. All that is necessary is to replace the variables by their expectations on the right, to specify the residuals accordingly, and to leave the
parameters the same. The interdependent system then takes the form of
conditional expectations, and thereby allows causal interpretation of the
parameters in the sense of inference (3). The causal variables, however,
are not the observed variables but the expected values of those variables;

that is the whole difference. Or not quite, for it so happens that the re-specification not only opens the door for a causal interpretation of the individual parameters of the system, but also for a substantial generaliz-ation of the approach. We get rid of the cumbersome assumption that each residual is uncorrelated with all of the predetermined variables of the system. In the generalized system each residual is assumed to be un-correlated with the explanatory equations of the same relation, and with nothing else, just as in ordinary regression.

Summing up, we can now see why I have referred to the models under 'choice of regression' and 'simultaneous equations' as involving a high degree of information: they are designed to allow numerical-operative inference in the causal sense (3). This is so whether we specify the relationship as linear or by way of some other parametric function $f(x)$. I take this opportunity to comment on the discussion between Kendall and Ehrenberg.[1] In a situation where we do not have information at all, I think it is a little unfair to describe a tentative specification as a dustbin approach. Such an attempt probably does no harm and may do some good. It may be necessary to spend years trying out all kinds of methods of formulating models before attaining success. Moreover, I like the com-parison with Newton's law of gravitation which, in a sense, is a model that is still unexplained but nonetheless works in the sense that we can use it to determine planetary motions.

Another more recent example is Pareto's law concerning the distribu-tion of wealth. It is no criticism of Pareto that he could not explain why this law holds; it is nevertheless useful.[2] I therefore agree with Ehrenberg that we should not confine ourselves to use merely what he calls the dustbin approach but I think we should not exclude from consideration many different types of models, some of which may be a little indefinite in specification.

Finally I am coming to the third stumbling block. The general point I wish to make here is that there is a tendency in econometric model building to operate with exact (residual-free) relationships in a formal manner, with the risk of running into the pitfall that the formal operations may sometimes be unrealistic. If we consider, for example, the case of income and expenditure, the hypothesis is that when income changes up and down the demand changes according to a single curve. Now this is a doubtful assumption and I am illustrating the difficulty by reference to a

---

[1] This is one of the time-honoured matters of debate in econometrics; reference is made to the illuminating discourse by Koopmans, Ref. 9.

[2] In a model by Whittle—Wold, Ref. 27, the Pareto parameter α comes out as the ratio between the growth rate of wealth and the mortality rate.

physical analogy. The so-called hysteresis loop, familiar in textbooks of physics, representing the relationship between electric current and induced magnetism, allows for the fact that, when the force increases, the magnetism increases along one curve but that, when the electric force decreases, the magnetism returns but not along the same curve. Something of a similar kind may apply in income distribution; for example, when people receive higher incomes they increase their standard of living, and then if income decreases they are naturally reluctant to see a decrease in their standard and so the relationship between income and incentive may be of the hysteresis loop kind. There therefore may not exist a single relationship independent of the direction of movement of the independent variable. There is nothing particularly novel about this argument, and it would agree with Milton Friedman's theory about 'permanent income'; it does, however, raise some new points in the specification of the model.

A second example is perhaps more novel, namely the question about reversibility in macro-models that are specified in terms of instrument and target variables. Incidentally, Professor Phillips, in his following paper, refers to these notions as decision variables and policy variables. I agree with the concept but I do not understand why he uses new terms for those which have been in current use for some ten years; the classical reference is Tinbergen (1956).

The problem may be illustrated in terms of financial policy. The government can use the interest rate as an instrument variable, and then money savings available for investment becomes the target variable. But after a while the government can change their policy and, for example, may not want to use government expenditure as an instrument in order to influence the rate of interest, which then becomes the target. The traditional theory would use the same relation in both cases, and where they switch a policy variable from instrument to target variable nothing happens to the model. This is rather a doubtful assumption. Again to take a physical analogy, the famous law in the theory of heat known as Carnot's circular process provides an instructive case in point. In the heat engine the circular process transforms heat H into work W, and the optimal efficiency is given by a proportionality relation $W = aH$. The reverse process makes the heat pump, which transforms work into heat, and here the optimal efficiency is a relation $W = bH$, the salient point being that b is smaller than the inverse of a. The lack of reversibility is due to the inevitable loss of energy when transforming heat into work, or conversely. In the same way in financial regulation there will be something analogous to heat losses and there is no reason why we should expect the same relationship between money volume and interest rate as between interest rate and money volume if in each case the former is the target variable.

One final comment. The other week I was considerably comforted by a discussion on this subject with one of my friends in Sweden, a Professor of Economics, who had independently arrived at the conclusion that the relationships between interest rates and money volume were not symmetrical. He thought there must be something wrong with his approach and had put his work away in a drawer for about three years but I think, as things have turned out, his analysis was sound.

References

[1] R. Bentzel and H. Wold (1946): On statistical demand analysis from the viewpoint of simultaneous equations. *Skandinavisk Aktuarietidskrift*, Vol. 29, 95-114.

[2] H. Cramér (1954): *The elements of probability theory and some of its applications.* Stockholm: Almqvist & Wiksell.

[3] H. Cramér and H. Wold (1935): Mortality variations in Sweden. A study in graduation and forecasting. *Skandinavisk Aktuarietidskrift*, Vol. 18, 161-241.

[4] M. Friedman (1953): *Essays in positive economics.* Chicago: Univ. Press.

[5] T. Haavelmo (1943): The statistical implications of a system of simultaneous equations. *Econometrica*, Vol. 11, 1-12.

[6] E.O. Heady and J.L. Dillon (1961): *Agricultural production functions.* Ames, Iowa: State University Press.

[7] L. Hurwicz (1950): Prediction and least squares. Pages 266-300 in *Statistical inference in dynamic economic models*, ed. T.C. Koopmans. New York: Wiley & Sons.

[8] M.G. Kendall (1951, 1952): Regression, structure and functional relationship. I-II. *Biometrika*, Vol. 38, 11-25; Vol. 39, 96-108.

[9] T.C. Koopmans (1957): *Three essays on the state of the economic science.* New York: Wiley & Sons.

[10] E.P. Mackeprang (1906): *Pristeorier.* Copenhagen: Bagge.

[11] H. Schultz (1938): *The theory and measurement of demand.* Chicago: Univ. Press.

[12] H. Theil (1958): *Economic forecasts and policy.* Amsterdam: North-Holland Publ. Co.

[13] J. Tinbergen (1939): *Statistical testing of business cycle theories.*
    I: *A method and its application to investment activity.*
    II: *Business cycles in the United States of America, 1919-1932.*
    Geneva: League of Nations.

[14] J. Tinbergen(1956): *Economic policy: Principles and design*. Amsterdam: North-Holland Publ. Co.

[15] H. Wold (1938): *A study in the analysis of stationary time series*. Uppsala: Almqvist & Wiksell. 2nd. ed. 1954.

[16] H. Wold (1956): Causal inference from observational data. A review of ends and means. *Journal of the Royal Statistical Society* (A), Vol. 119, 28-61.

[17] H. Wold (1961): Construction principles of simultaneous equations models in econometrics. *Bulletin of the International Statistical Institute*, Vol. 38, No. 4, 11-138.

[18] H. Wold (1965): Toward a verdict on macroeconomic simultaneous equations. Pages 115-166 in 'La semaine d'étude sur le rôle de l'analyse économétrique dans la formulation de plans de développement.' *Scripta Varia*, Vol. 28, Vatican City: Pontifical Academy of Sciences.

[19] H. Wold ed. (1965): *Bibliography on time series and stochastic processes*. Edinburgh: Oliver & Boyd.

[20] H. Wold (1966): Conclusions. Pages 319-321 in *Transactions des Entretiens de Monaco, 1964*. Monaco Centre International d'Étude des Problèmes Humains.

[21] H. Wold (1966): Nonlinear estimation by iterative least squares procedures. Pages 411-444 in *Festschrift Jerzy Neyman*, ed. F. David. New York: Wiley & Sons.

[22] H. Wold (1967): Time as the realm of forecasting. Pages 525-560 in *Interdisciplinary Perspectives of Times*. eds. E.M. Weyer and R. Fischer. New York: The New York Academy of Sciences.

[23] H. Wold (1967): Forecasting and scientific method. Paper in *Transactions of the Summer Institute on Forecasting on Scientific Basis, Curia 1966*. Lisbon: Gulbenkian Foundation. (In press.)

[24] H. Wold (1967): Cycles. Article in *International Encyclopedia of the Social Sciences*. New York: MacMillan. (In press.)

[25] H. Wold (1967): Nonlinear statistical analysis from the general point of view of scientific method. *Intern. Statist. Inst., Sydney session, Sept. 1967*.

[26] H. Wold in association with L. Juréen (1952), 1953): *Demand analysis. A study in econometrics*. Stockholm: Geber. New York: Wiley & Sons.

[27] H. Wold and P. Whittle (1957): A model explaining the Pareto distribution of wealth. *Econometrica*, Vol. 25, 591-595.

[28] G.U. Yule (1927): On a method of investigating periodicities in disturbed series, with special reference to Wolfer's sunspot numbers. *Phil. Trans. Roy. Soc.*, Vol. 226, 267-298.

MODELS FOR THE CONTROL OF ECONOMIC FLUCTUATIONS

A. W. PHILLIPS

For the last two decades the Governments of most Western countries have
been carrying out some degree of conscious control over their economies
with the purpose of overcoming the severe fluctuations in the general
level of economic activity and employment which plagued all free-enterprise
countries for a century or more before the first world war and which reached
catastrophic proportions in the inter-war years. A fair degree of success has
been achieved. In Britain the range of variation in unemployment since the
last war has been about two percent, compared with about ten percent in
the typical cycles of the century before the first world war and more than
twenty percent in the inter-war period. The range of the percentage variation in total output about its trend has, however, been greater; about eight
percent, or four times that of unemployment. This degree of success is
probably sufficient to permit the survival of free-enterprise economic
systems and democratic forms of government, but further improvement is
clearly desirable.

The results of research in model building and econometric estimation
are being used by Government Departments, though as yet in a rather
rudimentary way, in the practical task of controlling economic fluctuations.
Little if any use seems to have been made, however, of systematic methods
of decision analysis, although the linear decision rule method of analysis,
developed by Theil and others [2, 11] in Holland and independently by
Holt and others [4, 5] in the United States (and similar to the method developed independently by Kalman and others [6] for the control of chemical
processes) has been available for some years. My first purpose is to give
an outline of this method and the way it would be used in economic control. I then briefly indicate an inherent limitation of the method and state
the need for developing improved computational methods in order to facilitate the use of methods of learning or adaptive control.

Let the vector x_t be the set of values given in time-period t to the
variables over which the government has complete control and which it
uses to influence the economy. We will refer to these as decision variables.
In practice they may include such quantities as tax rates, hire purchase
deposit percentages and repayment times, investment allowances and grants,

and a number of monetary and financial quantities. Let the vector y_t be the set of values taken by other variables in which the government has a policy interest, but which it can influence only through its control of the decision variables. We shall call these the policy variables. They will include the percentage unemployment, the price level and its rate of change, the balance of payments on current account, the level of foreign reserves and perhaps other variables. If more disaggregated policy objectives are specified some of these quantities may themselves be vectors, for example the percentage unemployment in different regions or sectors and indices of prices of various broad classes of goods and services.

The values of the policy variables will depend not only on the values of the decision variables, but also on others, which can be classified into three sets; non-policy endogenous variables, which both influence and are influenced by the policy variables, exogenous variables, which influence the policy variables but are not influenced by them, and unobservable 'disturbances', which affect the system but are assumed to be unaffected by it. The number of truly exogenous variables is small; strictly perhaps only physical phenomena such as weather come into this category. However variables such as incomes and price levels for other countries are approximately exogenous and for practical purposes may often be treated as if they were truly exogenous. Some approximate decomposition of this kind is forced upon us if we are to avoid treating the whole world as a single system.

An econometric model is a mathematical representation of the way in which the policy and non-policy endogenous variables depend on one another and on the decision variables, exogenous variables, and disturbances. A considerable amount of experience in setting up, estimating and testing such models has now been accumulated, particularly in the United States, Holland, and more recently in Japan. The only model so far available for Britain is the one developed at Oxford by Klein, Ball, Hazlewood and Vandome [7], and recently modified and re-estimated by Professor Ball at the London Graduate School of Business Studies.

For the purpose of decision analysis the non-policy endogenous variables are irrelevant. They can be eliminated from the econometric model by the usual mathematical procedures, giving a reduced system showing the dependence of the policy variables on the decision variables, exogenous variables, and disturbances. The reduced system will be in the form of a system of difference equations. If these are not already linear in the variables and parameters they can, by further approximation, be converted into a linear system, which may be written in the general form

$$\sum_{r=0}^{a} A_r y_{t-r} + \sum_{r=0}^{b} B_r x_{t-r} + \sum_{r=0}^{c} C_r z_{t-r} + d_r + \sum_{r=0}^{m} M_r e_{t-r} = 0, \quad (1)$$

where A_o and M_o are unit matrices, y_t is the vector of policy variables, x_t the vector of decision variables, z_t is the vector of exogenous variables, d_t is a vector of constants or trend terms and e_t is a vector of serially uncorrelated random variables with zero means. Numerical estimates of the matrices A_r, B_r, C_r, and M_r, the scalers a, b, c and m, the parameters of the trend terms d_t, and the variance matrix of the random vector e_t can be calculated from estimates of the parameters of the econometric model. Alternatively if certain identification conditions are satisfied these values can be estimated directly from past observations of y_t, x_t, and z_t using methods due to Phillips [9].

The estimated reduced system (1) gives an approximate representation of the effects on the policy variables y_t of alternative choices of the decision variables x_t. To make further progress it is necessary to have a clear quantitative specification of the objectives of policy, or targets, and a criterion function giving the cost or disutility of deviations of the actual values of the variables from their target values. Although these are fundamental requirements of any rational process of decision making, those responsible for the decisions are usually reluctant even to admit the need for them, and still more reluctant to engage in the intellectually difficult and politically hazardous task of actually specifying quantitative objectives and a criterion of performance. In economic control the most immediate gains from analysis of the decision problem will probably come, as they have in other fields of operational research, from inducing policy makers to state these quantities more clearly.

There are immense computational advantages in dealing with a criterion which is quadratic in the variables involved, and we shall assume that the criterion can be adequately approximated by this form of function. Let $\bar{y}_t$ and $\bar{x}_t$ denote target values of the variables, and let $q_t (y_t, \bar{y}_t, x_t, \bar{x}_t)$ be a quadratic function giving the cost, or disutility, in period t of deviations from target values. Let Q_T be the present value of the total cost over periods 1 to T, where the next decision to be made is that for the period $t = 1$, and T, the decision horizon, is fairly large. Then if W_t is the present value of unit cost in a future period t, Q_T is given by

$$Q_T = \sum_{t=1}^{T} W_t \, q_t \qquad (2)$$

If the future values of the exogenous variables and disturbances were known, an optional sequence of decisions could be calculated by choosing the x_t, $t = 1, 2, \ldots, T$, to minimize Q_T subject to the constraints imposed by (1). Since Q_T is quadratic and the constraints are linear, the solutions can be obtained by straightforward methods of linear algebra. (See, for example, Theil, [11], especially chapter 4).

Since the future of the exogenous variables and disturbances will not be known we cannot in fact choose the x_t to minimize Q_T. The best we can do is to choose the x_t to minimize the mathematical expectation of Q_T conditional upon the information available in period O. Since differentiation and the taking of mathematical expectations are linear operations the order of carrying out these operations can be reversed, the differentiation being done first. We are thus led to a solution for the optimal decision sequence which is the same as would have been obtained if the future values of the exogenous variables and disturbances had been known, except that these future values are replaced by their conditional expectations, which are the same as their minimum-variance forecasts. This property of linear systems with quadratic criteria is known as the principle of certainty equivalence. The first term in the decision sequence is the optimal decision set for period one, the remaining terms are present best estimates of what the future decisions will be. But before each succeeding decision is taken new information will have become available enabling improved forecasts to be made and used. It turns out, however, that the same equation or decision rule holds for each time period. All that is necessary is to raise the time-subscripts of all variables by unity and insert the most recent forecasts.

There is no difficulty in obtaining forecasts of the disturbances. The random variables e_t in (1) are serially uncorrected with zero means, and it follows that the conditional expectations of all future e_t are zero. Forecasts of the exogenous variables z_t may be obtained in a variety of ways. A purely statistical forecasting procedure is to fit to past observations, say for $t = -N, \ldots., 0$, the mixed autoregressive moving average model

$$\sum_{r=0}^{g} G_r z_{t-r} + k_t = \sum_{r=0}^{h} H_r \epsilon_{t-r}, \quad G_0 = 1, \ H_0 = 1, \quad (3)$$

where G_r and H_r are matrices, k_t is a vector of constants or polynomials of low degree representing trend terms and the ϵ_t are serially uncorrected random vectors with zero means. The method due to Phillips [9] can be used to fit the model, giving estimates of the parameters and of past values of the vectors ϵ_t. Since the conditional expectations of future vectors ϵ_t are zero, forecasts of z_t are obtained by putting $\epsilon_t = 0$ for $t > 0$ and using the fitted model to calculate successively the forecast values of $z_1, \ldots, z_T$.

The solution for the optimal decision rule for the system (1) is of the form

$$\sum_{r=1}^{a} A^*_r y_{t-r} + \sum_{r=0}^{b} B^*_r x_{t-r} + V_t = 0, \quad B^*_0 = 1 \quad (4)$$

where V_t is a linear combination of the targets $\overline{y}_s$ and $\overline{x}_s$, the trend terms d_s and the forecast values of the exogenous variables z_s for $s = t, t + 1,$ ..., $t + T - 1$ and also of the initial values of z_s for $s = t - c, ..., t - 1$ and of e_s for $s = t - m, ..., t - 1$. If the decision rule is used for determining the values of x_t in successive periods t, equations (4) and (1) become two sub-systems forming a single system, and we immediately note an important possibility, that when control is being applied in strict accordance with (4) the sub-system (1) may no longer be identified. By this we mean that new observations generated by the operation of the complete system may give no further information by which to improve the estimates of the parameters of the sub-system (1). (The concept of identification is treated in texts on econometrics, for example Malinvaud [8]).

The possibility of lack of identification can be illustrated by considering the case in which the targets are constants and the exogenous variables are not serially correlated, so that their forecasts are constants. Then the vector V_t involves only a constant vector and the variables $z_{t - c}, ...,$ $z_{t - 1}; e_{t - m}, ..., e_{t - 1}$, all of which quantities occur also in the last three terms of (1). Moreover all the variables entering into the first two terms of (4) are also included in the first two terms of (1). Any scaler equation in (1) may therefore be replaced by any linear combination of itself and any scaler equation in (4) without change of form. Such a transformation leaves the statistical properties of the complete system unchanged, and it follows that none of the equations in (1) can be re-estimated directly from observations generated by the operations of the complete system.

In general the possibility of re-estimating the subsystem (1) from observations generated by the complete system will depend on the detailed structure of the model. I shall mention three factors which may lead to identification and so permit re-estimation. (a) The reduced system (1) is derived from a wider structural model by elimination of non-policy endogenous variables. It is possible that the equations of the structural model may be identified even though those of the reduced system (1) are not. (b) *A priori* specification may be sufficient to give identification of the equations in the reduced system itself. This will be so, for example, if there is a one-period time lag in the response of the system to the decision variables, so that B_0 in (1) is zero. (c) In practice the control is not likely to be applied exactly in accordance with the calculated rule (4), so that another disturbance vector will be added to (4), which may be independent of the disturbance vector in (1) and lead to identification of the equations in (1). The disturbances added to (4) may of course be deliberately applied for the purpose of obtaining better estimates of the system, and are then referred to as probes or perturbations.

The possibility that operation of the control may prevent re-estimation of the system should lead us to ask whether the decision analysis we have been considering does not have some fundamental deficiency. And indeed it has. The basic defect is simply that in deriving the decision rules no account was taken of the fact that the parameters of the system are not known exactly, and no consideration was given to ways in which we can improve our knowledge of the system while we are controlling it. In my view it cannot be too strongly stated that in attempting to control economic fluctuations we do not have the two separate problems of estimating the system and of controlling it, we have a single problem of jointly controlling and learning about the system, that is, a problem of learning control or adaptive control.

There is already a fairly extensive literature on methods of adaptive control, some of which are cited in Bellman [1]. The subject is closely related to the Bayesian approach to statistical decision theory as developed by Raiffa and Schlaiffer [10]. There is no major difficulty in principle in deriving an optimal learning or adaptive control for the type of system we have described; the major obstacle is that the function to be minimized is no longer quadratic so that the simple methods of linear algebra cannot be used to solve for the sequence of decision vectors. Numerical solutions have been obtained for extremely simple systems. (See, for example, Florentin [3]), but for all but the simplest cases the computational difficulties have so far proved insuperable. Further computational advances will be needed before practical procedures of optimal learning control can be divised for a problem as complex as that of the control of economic fluctuations.

References

[1] Bellman, Richard. *Adaptive Control Processes: A Guided Tour.* Princeton 1961.

[2] Van den Bogaard P.J.M. and Theil H., 'Macrodynamic Policy-Making: An Application of Strategy and Certainty Equivalence to the Economy of the United States 1933-36,' Metroeconomica XI (1959), 149-67.

[3] Florentin, J.J. 'Optimal, Probing, Adaptive Control of a Simple Bayesian System,' Control Section, Institution of Electrical Engineers, London, 1962.

[4] Holt, Charles C. 'Linear Decision Rules for Economic Stabilisation and Growth,' *Quarterly Journal of Economics* (1962), 20-45.

[5] Holt, C.C., Modigliani, F., Muth, J.F., and Simon, H.A. *Planning Production, Work Force and Inventories*, Prentice Hall, 1960.

[6] Kalman, R.E., Lapidees, L., and Shapiro, E., 'On the Optimal Control of

Chemical and Petroleum Processes' Symposium on Instrumentation and Computation. Institution of Chemical Engineers, London, May 1959.

[7] Klein, L.R., Ball, R.J., Hazlewood, A., and Vandome, P. *An Econometric Model of the U.K.*, Oxford, Blackwell 1961.

[8] Malinvaud, E. *Statistical Methods of Econometrics*, North Holland Publishing Co., Amsterdam, 1966.

[9] Phillips, A.W. *Estimation of Systems of Difference Equations with Moving Average Disturbances*, to be published.

[10] Raiffa, H., and Schlaiffer, R. *Applied Statistical Decision Theory*, Harvard, 1961.

[11] Theil, H. *Optimal Decision Rules for Government and Business*, North Holland Publishing Co., Amsterdam, 1964.